1/10/01

1/11
2

The Enchanted Wood
and Other Tales
from Finland

World Folklore Advisory Board

Simon J. Bronner, Ph.D.
Distinguished Professor of Folklore and American Studies
Pennsylvania State University at Harrisburg

Joseph Bruchac, Ph.D.
Abenaki Storyteller and Writer

Natalie O. Kononenko, Ph.D.
Professor of Slavic
Language and Literature
University of Virginia

Norma J. Livo, Ed.D.
Writer and Storyteller

Margaret Read MacDonald, Ph.D.
King County Library System

The Enchanted Wood
and Other Tales
from Finland

Norma J. Livo
George O. Livo

Photographs by Lauren J. Livo,
Steve Wilcox, and Denise Livo

1999
Libraries Unlimited, Inc.
Englewood, Colorado

LIBRARIES UNLIMITED, INC.
P.O. Box 6633
Englewood, CO 80155-6633
1-800-237-6124
www.lu.com

Library of Congress Cataloging-in-Publication Data

Livo, Norma J., 1929-
   The enchanted wood and other tales from Finland / by Norma J.
Livo, George O. Livo ; photographs by Lauren J. Livo, Steve Wilcox,
and Denise Livo ; cover art by Akseli Gallen-Kallela ; line drawings by
Joan Garner.
   xvii, 224 p.   19x26 cm. -- (World folklore series)
   Includes bibliographical references and index.
   ISBN 1-56308-578-X
   1. Tales--Finland. I. Livo, George O. II. Livo, Lauren J.
III. Wilcox, Steve. IV. Livo, Denise. V. Gallen-Kallela, Akseli.
VI. Garner, Joan. VII. Title. VIII. Series.
GR200.L575 1998
398.2'094897--dc21   98-23358
                                CIP

Dedicated to the newest generation of Livo Finns:
Jody, Todd, Davin,
Emily, Kurt, Andrea,
and Brooke

World Folklore Series

Folk Stories of the Hmong: Peoples of Laos, Thailand, and Vietnam. By Norma J. Livo and Dia Cha.

Images of a People: Tlingit Myths and Legends. By Mary Helen Pelton and Jacqueline DiGennaro.

Hyena and the Moon: Stories to Tell from Kenya. By Heather McNeil.

The Corn Woman: Stories and Legends of the Hispanic Southwest. Retold by Angel Vigil. Translated by Juan Francisco Marín and Jennifer Audrey Lowell.

Thai Tales: Folktales of Thailand. Retold by Supaporn Vathanaprida. Edited by Margaret Read MacDonald.

In Days Gone By: Folklore and Traditions of the Pennsylvania Dutch. By Audrey Burie Kirchner and Margaret R. Tassia.

From the Mango Tree and Other Folktales from Nepal. By Kavita Ram Shrestha and Sarah Lamstein.

Why Ostriches Don't Fly and Other Tales from the African Bush. By I. Murphy Lewis.

The Magic Egg and Other Tales from Ukraine. Retold by Barbara J. Suwyn. Edited and with an Introduction by Natalie O. Kononenko.

Jasmine and Coconuts: South Indian Tales. By Cathy Spagnoli and Paramasivam Samanna.

When Night Falls, Kric! Krac! Haitian Folktales. By Liliane Nérette Louis. Edited by Fred Hay, Ph.D.

A Tiger by the Tail and Other Stories from the Heart of Korea. Retold by Lindy Soon Curry. Edited by Chan-eung Park.

The Enchanted Wood and Other Tales from Finland. By Norma J. Livo and George O. Livo.

The Eagle in the Cactus: Traditional Stories from Mexico. By Angel Vigil.

Selections Available on Audiocassette

Hyena and the Moon: Stories to Listen to from Kenya. By Heather McNeil.

The Corn Woman: Audio Stories and Legends of the Hispanic Southwest. English and Spanish versions. By Angel Vigil. Spanish version read by Juan Francisco Marín.

Thai Tales: Audio Folktales from Thailand. By Supaporn Vathanaprida and Margaret Read MacDonald. Narrated by Supaporn Vathanaprida. Produced and with an Introduction by Margaret Read MacDonald.

Folk Tales of the Hmong: Audio Tales from the Peoples of Laos, Thailand, and Vietnam. By Norma J. Livo and Dia Cha.

National Anthem

Oi maamme Suomi synnyinmaa,
soi sana kultainen.
::Ei laaksoa, ei kukkulaa,
ei vetta rantaa rakkaampaa,
kuin kotimaa taa pohjoinen,
maa kallis isien.::

Land of Suomi, my native land,
Oh the ring of that golden word,
::No vale or hilly stand,
No dearer waters or foaming strand,
As my northern homeland here,
Land our fathers held dear.::

Contents

Part I
FOLKLIFE

Part II
FOLKLORE

Part III
RECIPES

Part IV
REFERENCES, BIBLIOGRAPHY, AND INDEX

Foreword

As the son of Finnish immigrant parents who came to the United States at the turn of the century, I have spent considerable time reading, watching, listening to, and observing things about my Finnish heritage.

In reading this book I have found a single source that spans the time frame from the ice age to present-day Finland in terms of its people, lifestyles, struggles, achievements, and its cherished folklore.

This book is presented in a very easy to read and comprehensible format that I recommend for anyone who might be interested in learning about Finland's history and traditions.

Needless to say, the folklore portion of this book was exciting to read, hard to put down, and allowed the mind to remember those wonderful times when fairy tales were an important part of each day.

As the folklore portion ended and I discovered the recipe section, my mouth began to water and I could smell and taste the wonderful delicacies my mother used to prepare (lutefisk excepted), some fifty years since.

I hope you find this book as interesting, informative, and educational as I did, and whether your goal is learning about your heritage or just about Finland and its history, you will enjoy the pleasant ride through time, in fact and fiction.

In conclusion I want to thank the authors, Norma and George Livo for their untiring efforts throughout the years, and now with this book, in sharing with us their knowledge and experience of Finland, the Finns, their history, lifestyles, hopes, and dreams. Your contributions are greatly enjoyed and appreciated.

Daniel L. Kamunen
Consul of Finland

Acknowledgments

We are grateful to the parents of George O. Livo. His mother, Alli Hedvig Ala-Koukkari Livo, served in the Lotta Svard (the women's auxiliary organization) during the intense struggle for Finnish Independence. His father, Pekka Livo, served with the partisans in their losing struggle to gain independence for Karelia.

Pekka's sisters Irene and Vappu are part of the book. Vappu Karjalainen was forced to dig Russian fortifications in the winter with no more than rags for shoes. She was one of the ill-clothed, ill-fed multitudes during this war in Karelia against Finnish forces.

Irene's daughters Inkeri Saha and Kyllikki Kangas are also an important part of this book on Finland. Kyllikki's husband Aare Kangas armed with molotov cocktails, faced Russian tanks on the Karelian Isthmus.

Cousins Anna-Liisa and Erkki Koppelomaki took us around much of Finland on a memorable tour-de-force full of people, stories, and sights. Cousins Matti and Sirkka Ylinen and family, cousins Aare and Maija Kivineva, and their son Esa and his wife Eija Kivineva shared family history and legends.

Our daughter Lauren accompanied us on our trip to Finland, Sweden, and Estonia in 1995. A herpetologist, photographer, and writer, she enabled us to see Finland and family from a new perspective. Her enthusiasm enriched the whole trip.

We are also grateful for the gracious hospitality of Juhani and Aino Ala-Koukkari and family, and Mariaana and Jarmo Malkakorppi. There were many others who shared memories, stories, and experiences with us.

Further thanks go to the Finnish Embassy for supplying brochures, books, and many booklets on the Finns and to Honorary Consul of Finland, Dan Kamunen for his support and reactions.

And finally, our thanks to Susan Zernial, Barbara Ittner, and Kevin W. Perizzolo of Libraries Unlimited who encouraged and honed our efforts. To all, *kiitos*!

Introduction

Finland is a beautiful country full of creative, vigorous, hard-working, warm, and mischievous people. Not enough is known in the United States about this quiet country and its folk-glue; the authors hope this book will help fill that void. It includes information about Finland's geology, history, people, traditions, and arts and crafts, as well as the contributions of Finns in the United States. Also in the book are folklore, folktales, and favorite Finnish recipes.

We hope that children with Finnish roots may find some of their own special interests here. All young readers should be able to see how these stories are unique to Finland, yet how they encompass all of humanity.

The Enchanted Wood and Other Tales from Finland is intended for use by educators, librarians, and students as well as the general public.

Family picture.

Part I

Folklife

1

Introduction to Suomi (Finland)
The Home of *Sisu*

Introduction

Come, let us lead you into the magical woods of Finland, and through the beguiling and bewitching power of the marvelous tales and fantastic legends of the Finns. Here in their endless green forests still dwell the shy illusive woodspirits, trolls, and gnomes, ruled over by the all-pervasive and powerful forest god Tapiola. Let us introduce you to the stories and extensive folklore of this small nation of innovative people. Come with us to the north woods and meet the people with *SISU*.

Sisu means guts, tenacity, and perseverance, often in the face of great odds or adversity. People living in northern climates need plenty of *sisu*. There they eke out an existence in a glaciated hardscrabble land with a brief, if glorious, growing season coupled with a long dark winter. Nights can be eerily ablaze with the ghostly dance of the northern lights—spirits of the dead, many believe.

The summers are short, but they make up for it with incredible long days called "white nights." Even at midnight there is a ghostly twilight with the sun on the horizon peering out from behind the ever-present evergreens, casting long spooky shadows across the landscape. Dark shadows seem to flit among the trees—who could be lurking, watching, waiting?

Come meet the Finns. Let us start at the very beginning, with the legendary birth of the universe as taken from the great Finnish national epic *The Kalevala* (*The Land of Heroes*).

The Fantastic Kalevala *Creation Myth*

The birth of the cosmos in the ancient Finnish *Kalevala* creation myth occurs when the beautiful virgin maiden Ilmatar, goddess of the air, becomes bored. She descends from the vast empty spaces of the heavens to the endless sea surface. A strong windstorm rises in the east and sweeps the churning whitecapped sea into a frothy foam. The sea-foam impregnates the air-goddess. Her pregnancy lasts an incredible 700 years—nine ages of humans.

This exceedingly long gestation becomes very uncomfortable for Ilmatar; she swims and drifts hither and yon with the child still unborn. Suffering in her condition, she regrets leaving the high empty spaces. Weeping softly, she calls out to Ukko (the ancient god of thunder), the supreme lord of all, to release her from her misery. Time passes. Then a scaup (a golden-eyed diving duck) flies around vainly searching for a nesting site in the endless bluish sea. Taking pity on the scaup, the goddess raises her shoulder and knee out of the sea. The goldeneye, mistaking the knee for a grassy tussock, builds her nest on it.

In the nest, the scaup lays six golden eggs, then a seventh of iron. She broods the eggs. After three days the heat generated on the goddess's knee becomes unbearable. Ilmatar twitches her leg, jerking the eggs out of the nest. The eggs roll into the sea and shatter. Magically they do not mix with the water or bottom mud but transform into beautiful and marvelous things. One egg's lower half becomes the earth below, while the upper half of its shell becomes the dome of the sky. The yellow yolk of this egg becomes the sun, and the white gathers into the pale moon. The mottling on the shell and other brighter bits of the eggs form the stars, and the darker parts make up the clouds.

After nine years, in the tenth summer, the maiden Ilmatar raises her head from the seas, and, thrashing about with her body, hands, and feet, she creates headlands, hollows, salmon haunts, bays, and reefs. She finishes her creation by raising islands, then the mainlands. Thus Finland and the continents rise from the waters of the sea.

Meanwhile, steadfast old Vainamoinen, the eternal bard and wizard, stays another 30 years in his mother Ilmatar's womb meditating. Finally he is born and falls headfirst into the sea, where he is tossed about by the billows for another 8 years. He emerges from the waves to stand on the headland of an island with no name and no trees. (Finland, as it rose from the Baltic Sea, was a barren waste strewn with glacial boulders and debris.)

Vainamoinen lingers many years just considering and pondering. Who is to sow this land and make it fruitful? He conjures up Sampsa Pellervoinen, the field's son, who sows the lands and swamps with plants such as grasses, heather, willows, alders, chokecherries, junipers, firs, ash, pines, spruce, and oaks. The World Tree, the oak, grows so big and tall that it reaches the clouds and shades out the other plants. It must be cut to allow the sun to shine.

With the help of his mother, Vainamoinen conjures up from the sea a thumb-sized man clad in a copper hat, boots, mittens, and belt, and carrying a copper ax. Vainamoinen berates the little man for being so tiny. A puny creature only as high as an ox's hoof can hardly be expected to tackle the World Oak! At that insult the man grows to enormous stature, so large that his eyes are a fathom apart and his head touches the clouds! The giant sharpens his now-huge ax with six whetstones. He steps up to the root of the tree and, with fire flashing from the ax, swings the blade three times into the trunk of the tree. On the third stroke, the huge oak comes crashing down. The boughs, leaves, and chips float off to sea spreading their magic. The sun is now able to shine on the land, and farming (slash-and-burn) is able to start.

The Cosmology (as science sees it, and it is just as fantastic)

Interesting aspects of the birth of the universe as well as the geology of Finland can be compared to the creation myth of the ancient Finns. Our goal is not to delve in any great depth into astronomy or the extremely ancient and complex geology of Finland, as this is a book on folklore, but to touch on some intriguing parallels between scientific facts (as far as we know them) and mythology.

On their incredible journey to the moon, our valiant astronauts were awestruck when they viewed our Earth from their vantage point in space. Planet Earth shines as a wondrous blue jewel in the deep velvety void. To think that a golden-eyed scaup laid this blue egg! What a contrast our beautiful planet makes next to her barren, desolate, lifeless moon, so cratered and pockmarked.

Scientists say that the universe started with the Big Bang. The Blue Egg was even smaller than our scaups, yet all the cosmos fit into it! Talk about togetherness. Their egg, also smashed, is still flying apart as receding galaxies. Our Sun is in one of the spiral arms of the Milky Way Galaxy nestled among the younger stars.

The Solar System started as a whirling disc of gas and dust. The debris came from older stars that had gone supernova and exploded. The Sun's gravity gathered in 99 percent of the material of the disc, leaving enough to form the nine planets and assorted asteroids, comets, and meteorites. Our Sun is a nuclear reactor. The hydrogen in the Sun's core is squeezed by the enormous pressure of overlying layers and is extremely hot. This results in fusion as the hydrogen atoms smash together to form helium and give off enormous energy. Radiation from the Sun makes life on Earth possible.

The Earth became a molten ball almost 8,000 miles in diameter, and as in a blast furnace the heavy materials, especially iron, sank to form a massive core. This core is mostly molten, with a small solid center. It forms a yolk for the Earth egg (semi-hard-boiled). Above the core is the thick mantle, the white of the egg! It is made of very hot rocks that are near the melting point only a hundred miles down.

A forty mile or so thick crust of lighter rocks overlies the mantle. This crust is broken just like an eggshell, into large shards called plates. These plates slide around on the hot mantle, carrying the continents on their backs. New crust is formed from upwelling molten lava along fracture zones, and old crust is pushed into the hot mantle and melted at what are called subduction zones. This process is called Plate Tectonics. The plates move around like ice on a pond or scum on a seething pot.

Finland sits on a modest-sized plate called Baltica, which includes parts or all of some surrounding countries. It has been on an incredible journey since it formed about 3 billion years ago. In its geological history it moved from the Arctic to the Equator, then down to the Antarctic, and back north again. It crawled with the first amphibians, and later had tree ferns and dinosaurs! Quite a story for an old pile of rock.

The Ice Age came to Finland some 2 million years ago. Snow accumulated in the mountains between Sweden and Norway and formed glaciers that swept west into the North Sea and carved out the magnificent fjords of Norway. To the east, they pushed across Sweden and filled the Gulf of Bothnia. The continent-sized glacier pushed like a gigantic bulldozer carrying a vast load of sand, gravel, and boulders, southeast across Finland. Four major ice advances have been mapped, but sea floor sediments suggest as many as eighteen. The younger advances tended to destroy the geological evidence of the previous ones.

Two large parallel glacial terminal moraines of debris formed broad arcs across southeastern Finland. There the ice margin stood for many years as the rate of ice advance and the melting rate of the ice margin were in equilibrium. But the Ice Age came to an end about 12,000 years ago as rapid melting took place. The ice had scraped and scoured the land with the debris it carried, and when it melted it left polished rock surfaces on a largely granite terrain. It also left behind sand and boulders and scooped-out hollows, plus a huge lake of fresh water (the Baltic Sea). Finland, for the most part, sank out of sight!

Here is where the *Kalevala* legend really shines. For at first there was only the sea of fresh water (later to become salty as the sea level worldwide rose and the Baltic Sea joined the North Sea south of Sweden). The land was hundreds of meters under water. Only wind and endless waves! The goddess of the air, Ilmatar, began kicking up the sea bottom, and the land began to rise. Here and there a few islands poked up. These grew in size and coalesced into larger land masses. More and more islands and shoals appeared as the land grew, uniting with the mainland to the east, towards Karelia (Karjala in Finnish). This process of emergence continues even today, particularly on the west of Finland, at about 3 feet (one meter) a century along the Gulf of Bothnia.

When the demigod Vainamoinen first stood on the rocky headland of an island, a land desolate beyond description, he saw a glacial landscape newly emerged; undoubtedly somewhat muddy from glacial clays. Life came with spores and seeds carried by the wind and birds. First the northern mosses, lichens, willows, and other northern shrubs took root. Later evergreens and then finally deciduous trees arrived. Tundra formed in the far north. Many shallow lakes filled in and became swamps and muskeg. Others remained as sparkling blue jewels, connected by rushing streams.

The climate has varied until modern times, and we probably are not completely out of the Ice Age yet. If the ice in Antarctica melts and the sea level rises, low-lying Finland may again sink under the waves.

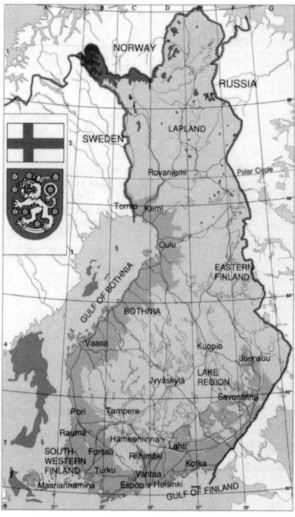

Total area:	338,145 sq. km. of which	Land frontiers:
	304,623 sq. km. land	
	33,522 sq. km. water	c. 3,671 km.
		(586 km. with Sweden,
Maximum length	1,160 km.	716 km. with Norway,
Maximum width	540 km.	1,269 km. with Russia)

Reprinted from *Focus on Finland* (Helsinki, Finland: Otava Publishing Co., 1995). Used by permission.

Land and Climate

Finland, with a population of a little more than 5 million people, is the fifth largest country in Europe in area. Lying at the extreme northern edge of Europe between latitudes 60 degrees N and 70 degrees N, it covers some 130,000 square miles. Almost one-half of the people living above the Arctic Circle are Finns. The southernmost point of Finland is north of Scotland and at about the middle of Hudson's Bay in North America. As in most of Scandinavia, the majority of Finns live in the south and southwestern parts of the country, where the climate and clay soil allow for a more extensive and varied type of agriculture.

Most of Finland is a relatively flat, low-lying, somewhat undulating peneplain. The country's fertile southwest part juts out as a large blunt peninsula into the Baltic Sea. To the west, the Gulf of Bothnia adjoins Sweden, and the Gulf of Finland is to the south, adjoining Finland's close linguistic cousin Estonia. To the northwest, the country borders Sweden and Norway. To the east, Finland has a 788-mile border with Russia (the largest country in the world in area). The highest elevations in Finland are located in the north and northwest and reach a maximum height of 4,370 feet (1,344 meters) above sea level.

Although a quarter of Finland's land surface lies above the Arctic Circle, its climate is modified somewhat by the Baltic Sea and especially by the warming west winds off the Gulf Stream. This equatorial current, originating in the Caribbean Sea and the Gulf of Mexico, flows past Florida into the Atlantic. Heading northeast across the Atlantic, it carries an enormous heat load in giant swirls. On its way, it warms Ireland and the British Isles before emptying into the North Sea off Norway and dissipating its remaining heat in the Arctic Ocean.

It is this warming by the Gulf Stream that makes Scandinavia habitable. Because of this warming, Finland is the most densely forested country in Europe. Its forests are referred to as "green gold." Evergreens cover much of Finland (and Sweden) except for a northern strip of lichens, moss, and scrub-covered tundra, where a year-round permafrost, a relic of the Ice Age, inhibits tree growth.

Because of the Gulf Stream, summer temperatures in southern Finland are similar to those in England and Holland. In northern Finland, the summer temperature averages about 4 or 5 degrees cooler than those of England and Holland. Winter temperatures in Finland in January usually range from 17-27 degrees F near Helsinki to 4-14 degrees F at the Arctic Circle at Rovaniemi. In rare years, a cold blast from Siberia has been known to plummet winter temperatures to as low as -40 degrees F (or C).

Daylight varies in the south of Finland from a minimum of about six hours during the winter to more than twenty hours in the summer. Above the Arctic Circle it is totally dark in midwinter except for starlight and the occasional appearance of the Aurora Borealis (Northern Lights). In midsummer the sun never sets; the country is bathed in sunlight 24 hours a day. People tend to "hibernate" more in the winter and get cabin fever. During summer, people stay up all hours and enjoy the outdoors.

The Arrival of People in Finland (Archaeology)

A reindeer culture of Lapps (Sami) was established in Finland as the Ice Age waned. Stone Age hunter-gatherers moved in early to fish and to hunt seals and other animals. Around 3000 BC the Comb-Ceramic culture appeared fully developed from the east and spread into Finland. These people decorated the bases of their pottery with a comb-like stamp, hence their name. The Comb-Ceramic people were the first inhabitants of Finland that were probably of the Finno-Ugric stock. They were still hunters and fishers whose only domestic animal was the dog. By this time, humans worldwide were capable of making and using boats. Chances are excellent that all the shores of the Gulf of Bothnia and much of the eastern Baltic were settled by these people. Remember that much of Finland and eastern Sweden was still rising from the sea.

The Comb-Ceramic people intermingled with a pre-Ceramic culture. Both used similar stone tools. Other migrations continued from the southern Baltic, especially from Estonia and the east.

Starting about 1800 BC, the Battle Ax culture (also known as the Cord-Ceramic culture) reached Finland, Sweden, and Norway, probably from the south. These peoples were long-skulled Indo-European types. They used boat-shaped battle axes and tended cattle, which seems to have been their most important activity, although they practiced some agriculture. They were excellent sailors and maintained active relations with the Swedish side of the Gulf of Bothnia. Their dead were buried with strict religious rituals and interred with tools, axes, and food in pottery for the next life.

The Battle Ax culture merged with the older resident culture and was oriented more to the west than the east. It became known (from burial sites) as the Kiukainen culture of 1600 to 1200 BC.

Bronze was introduced into Finland about 1300 BC from the west. Different types of bronze objects appeared from the east a few hundred years later. The coastal (trade) areas had bronze, but the interior still used bone and stone implements for hunting and fishing.

By 500 BC the climate turned cold and the population dwindled, probably migrating south. Later, the climate again warmed, and people returned by the end of the millennium.

Finnish was evidently spoken over a large area of eastern Europe, from the Arctic to the Black Sea, by a genetically diverse people. These people were displaced and dispersed by a great increase of Turkish and Slavic people to the south and east along the Silk Road. Hordes of so-called barbarians pushed west. Other waves of Finnish-speaking people had already reached the Baltic Sea a few hundred years before the end of the millennium. They pushed through Estonia into Karelia and Finland. These "Baltic" Finns merged with the earlier population in Finland. The Hungarians, a distant cousin of the Finns ethnically and linguistically, became completely separated from the Baltic Finns. These Hungarian horsemen pushed into central Europe, into the area they still inhabit.

The new Baltic Finn arrivals introduced the Iron Age to Finland and used local bog-iron ores to produce iron. Although the Baltic Finns numbered fewer than the resident population, their higher level of technology and culture allowed them to absorb the aboriginal inhabitants.

By the time Rome fell, and between AD 400-800, the Finns already had strong bonds with Sweden to the west. Both had a similar Iron Age culture, including boat burials of chiefs who had become a ruling class. In Finland, however, the boat was burned before entombment. Finnish folk poems describe such a burial as a "boat of bronze" from the remote heroic age.

Most of the agriculture at this time was of the slash-and-burn variety. Fields were cleared one year and burned the next, and the ashes were worked into the soil with a light plow among the tree stumps, which were left standing. (A similar agriculture is still practiced in parts of the world today.) Seeds were sown among the stumps. After a few good harvests the nutrients of the soil were depleted, and the area was allowed to return to forest. New areas were then cleared.

After the harvest and during the winter, the men trapped, hunted, and fished. They often traveled on long expeditions facilitated by the large system of interconnected waterways that occupied the glacier-scoured lowlands. Boats were rowed for scores of miles and portaged across short rapids. During the winter, sleighs were used over these frozen waterways. Luxurious northern furs (sable, fox, polar bear, seal, and walrus), down, and walrus ivory could be traded (through the Germans) all the way south to the populous Mediterranean world for luxury goods such as swords, salt, fine pottery, cloth, glass, and jewelry. Nearer to home, the women and children picked a variety of berries and mushrooms that were dried and stored to be used all winter.

By the eighth century, the Gulf of Finland had become part of an important trade route that wound its way through the Neva River to Lake Ladoga and hence through Russia, by the Dnieper to the Black Sea, and finally to the Arabian lands around the eastern Mediterranean. Viking expeditions from Sweden seeking trade and plunder followed this route. They probably included Finns from Ostrobothnia. The Vikings founded colonies along the way among the Finno-Ugric and Slavic peoples.

Meanwhile, Scandinavia came under the rule of kings. No unified state formed in Finland; it remained divided into fiercely independent clans who valued their freedom. The hinterland still remained a vast wilderness roamed by only hunters and Lapps (Sami). Organizations of trappers and armed trading associations formed to procure furs and collect tribute from the Lapps. By the end of the pagan period, three main regions of settlement had formed; one was in Karelia, and two were in Finland proper. Culturally, Finland was at the same level as Sweden, but much of Finland's culture had its origin in the Baltic areas to the south. Archaeology shows that this time was filled with turmoil. Fortified hilltops were places of refuge. An unbroken system of hilltop signal fires (warning of enemy attacks) has been found.

The richness of Finland's natural resources became a sought-after prize by the more organized states of Sweden and Novgorod. The Slavs had taken over the old Varangian trading centers formed under Swedish control. These united into Novgorod, the nucleus of what was to become the powerful state of Russia. At first Novgorod traded actively and peacefully with Finland. It apparently established a trading post in southwestern Finland near Turku. The importance of this trade is indicated by Turku being listed in an Arabian geography from AD 1154!

Sami, or Laplanders

There are two types of Sami (the name they prefer): the eastern type, who resemble northern Asian peoples, and the western type, who are closer to Europeans in heritage. It is believed that the original Sami people came to Finland and eastern Karelia during and after the last Ice Age. Nomads who followed the large herds of reindeer, the Sami were hunters and fishers. Some Sami lived in the forests and established villages, usually located by a large river. They lived in groups of families or clans. The Sami language probably developed through language exchange with early basic Finnish. It is now regarded as one of the Finno-Ugric languages.

Before we continue, a word about reindeer. The Sami domesticated the reindeer more than 3,000 years ago. Reindeer were necessary for transportation, furs, and clothing. So important were the reindeer to the Sami culture that there are about 400 names for reindeer according to gender, age, color, shape, etc. The term "reindeer" refers to the same animal known as the caribou in North America. The name comes from a Sami word meaning "animals that pasture" or "animal that eats plants off the ground." A reindeer weighs an average of 240 pounds. Reindeer are famous for their ability to eat lichen.

Back to the history of the Sami. Ghengis Khan wrote that the Sami were the one nation he would never try to fight again. This was because they were not warriors in the usual sense. They simply did not believe in war, so they disappeared in times of conflict. They are peaceful retreaters and have never been to war. They have an ability to adapt to changing conditions, whether those conditions are changed by people or nature. During the Middle Ages, when an agricultural population invaded the coastal area of Sweden and Finland, the Sami who had originally inhabited this area were pushed north so that now they can only be found north of the Arctic Circle.

The Sami created prehistoric works of stone-carved art found along coastlines. It is theorized that these works were carved by people with high social status, such as a shaman. The pictures probably were designed to influence nature or to call upon the spirits. Among them are boats, clubs, hunting equipment, skis, and snowshoes. People and animals were shown in profile.

The religion of the Sami was animistic with shamanistic features. They believed that all objects in nature had a spirit; therefore, everyone was expected to move quietly in the wilderness. Shouting and making a disturbance was not allowed. The Sami believed the dead lived on in spirit. Important places had their divinities, and every force of nature had its god. The Sami also believed in malicious gnomes, called *stallu*, which were thought to be large, strong, simple human-like beings living in the forest. A *stallu* always traveled with a dog who could sometimes steal a young Sami girl to become the gnome's wife.

Contact with the gods was the responsibility of the head of the family, who used his magic drum to talk to them. However, a person with a special gift could be called to become a *noaide* or shaman. Because of this special gift, people would come to the person for help and advice. The shaman was a link between the spiritual world and the people and could travel to the underworld or the upper spirit world.

The magic drum, or rune drum, called a *kannus*, is made of fir, pine or birch, but only from a tree that has grown in an isolated place out of reach of the sun. The tree must also be growing with a clockwise twist. Rawhide reindeer skin is stretched over the wooden drum base, and a piece of wood is used as a handle under the drum. Nine lines are painted on the drum with alder bark juice. The alder god ruled over the wild animals and held a high position; the bark of the alder mixed with spit provided fiery red juice used for painting the figures on the shaman's drum.

The Tree of Life is painted on the drum and rules all four directions of the universe. A *lovi* or hole is painted in the center of the drum; it leads from one level of the universe to another. The drum also has all kinds of luck-bringing animals painted on it. Small rings of copper or bone are placed on the drum, and the shaman beats the drum with a hammer made from animal horn lined with beaver skin.

The drum was a portable altar. Stories tell that many shamans used to come together to beat the drum to see whose art was strongest. While the shaman beats the drum, he chants runic songs until he goes into a trance and travels to the other world. The copper piece hops around on the drum and finally stops on one of the lines. The action is much like that on a Ouija board. From this the shaman knows what will happen in the future.

When the Christian influence took hold, Sami people were converted to Christianity by force, and their shamanistic practices were forbidden. In spite of this ban, there is evidence that the Sami practiced elements of their original religion as late as the 1940s. However, many Sami were burned at the stake with their magic drums during the witch-hunting frenzy of the 1600s (much like Salem in the United States).

Sami Today

There are approximately 48,000 Sami in Norway, Sweden, Finland, and Russia. Currently the Sami are in the same predicament as the Native American peoples. They were pushed from their original territories and viewed with a patronizing attitude. However, in 1962-1963 an official policy stated that "the Sami-speaking population must be given the opportunity to preserve its language and other cultural customs on terms that accord with the expressed wishes of the Sami themselves."

The Sami have a flag, which was acknowledged officially in 1986. The basic symbolism on the flag is that of the drum head. The circle is a symbol of sun and moon. The sun ring is red while the moon ring is blue. These are the same colors used in Sami folk clothing.

Traditional Sami handicrafts include horn and wood carving, basketry, leather work, and making magic drums. Sami folk songs have won increasing recognition, illustrated by the fact that a Sami sang traditional songs in the opening ceremonies of the Lillehammer Olympics.

Many Sami women are the spokespersons for their families and may make important decisions on its behalf. It is not unusual for Sami women to keep their maiden names after marriage.

History

Beginnings with Sweden

By the end of the twelfth century a feeding frenzy of resources by the "wolves of the Baltic" (Swedes, Russians, Germans, and Danes) took place. The result was that the Teutonic Order (Germans) established trading colonies along the south shore of the Baltic Sea and took over this area. These colonies remained firmly in German hands until World War II.

Sweden and Finland more or less peacefully united for the next 600 or so years as the kingdom of Sweden-Finland. The Danes eventually pulled back from the eastern Baltic and from the provinces of southern Sweden because of the growing strength of Sweden. Norway, Denmark, and Sweden had intermittent wars during this period. Norway and Sweden joined at times but eventually separated.

Religion

Sweden was converted from paganism to Christianity beginning in the south in the early 800s. This process was finally completed in the eleventh century, when the last staunch pagan holdouts in northern Sweden became Christian.

A similar process occurred in Finland. Christianity arrived partly with trade from the west, but paganism retained its hold in the interior for several hundred years. Some pagan practices and magic evidently persisted into modern times.

Russia accepted Christianity around 988. In 1054, when the Catholic church split, Russia took the Eastern Orthodox side and eventually became known as the Russian Orthodox church. The rivalry between Sweden and Novgorod (Russia) was heightened by the religious breach between them. Both wanted to convert the Finns to their particular brand of Christianity. According to some sources some priests made trips to Finland, but the religion did not take hold. The Swedes, with the blessings of the Pope, embarked upon a "crusade" with both economic and religious objectives (mainly the former). Around 1157 King Eric landed with his small army somewhere in southwestern Finland. His troops easily routed the agricultural Finns.

After King Eric left that summer, an Englishman named Bishop Henry was left behind to organize the new church. Accounts differ as to what happened the following winter when Bishop Henry provoked a yeoman named Lalli. Apparently the Bishop took fodder and provisions from Lalli's farm without permission, although he did leave payment. Lalli, who was antagonistic toward the new religion, accosted the Bishop on frozen Lake Köyliö and during an argument killed the priest with an ax. Henry was buried near Turku. Within 50 years the church saw to it that he began to be revered as a saint. He is now St. Henry, the apostle of Finland. In addition, he is also one of the patron saints of Sweden.

The establishment of a bishop's office, organizing parishes and building churches, imposed a big financial burden on the new converts. This burden was onerous to the farmers who struggled to make a living in those northern hardscrabble conditions. Instead of treating the Finns as allies, the Pope urged Sweden to conquer Finland. This was a task easier said than done. Only the strip along the coast of the Gulf of Bothnia became Christianized in the following decades. The Swedes later mounted another "crusade" to Finland that was somewhat more successful. Still, paganism retained its hold in the interior for several hundred years. Some pagan practices and magic persisted into modern times.

Meanwhile, the Russians forcibly baptized all the Karelians they could, along with related tribes in Livonia, Ingria, and Estonia. The Danes established a trading beachhead in Finland along with missionaries. The Germans tried to dominate both sides of the Gulf of Finland and to gain control of the mouth of the strategic Neva River. However, they had strong competition from the Danes, Swedes, and Russians.

During the end of the Reformation in the 1500s, Lutheranism spread to Scandinavia, including Finland. This period of reformation took hold in Finland as Catholicism never had. Lutheranism became the state religion of Finland and remains so to this day.

Russia

Novgorod became Russia and expanded in various directions. The Russian Tsars wanted a warm water port and kept expanding towards the Black Sea. Turkey prevented them from taking the Dardanelles, thus stopping their expansion into the Mediterranean Sea area. During one of Russia's innumerable wars with Sweden-Finland, the Swedish Empire lost the province of Ingria, and the Russians captured the Finnish fort and town of Nevanlinna at the mouth of the Neva River in 1703. Here, in 1704, Peter the Great, the Russian Tsar, decided to build his capital. Because of this, the Finns have almost certainly lost this territory forever. (Not surprisingly, this area is the source of current border problems.)

Finland had the unenviable position of being the battleground for many of the wars fought between the powers vying for supremacy in the Baltic region (particularly those between Sweden and Russia). In the 263 years between 1500 and 1763, Sweden-Finland was at war with various countries and alliances around the Baltic more than half of the time. (Think of the enormous treasure and the multitude of lives lost or wrecked!) Well known for its tough fighting men, Finland supplied much of the cannon fodder and provisions for the often ill-advised and reckless ventures of Sweden-Finland, which stretched from the eastern Baltic through Poland and Saxony. During wars, the Finns did much of the fighting and dying while the majority of the officers were Swedish. Successful campaigns resulted in these Swedish officers often being rewarded with large tracts of land in Finland.

All parts of Finland were occupied at one time or another by Russian troops, who often raped, looted, and burned at will. The one occasion when Russian troops were in Sweden—as an ally during a war with Denmark—was enough of a taste of the Russians for the Swedes. The Swedish "Mother Country" escaped devastation by feeding Finland to the Russian Bear while Finnish troops were pulled into Sweden for "home" defense, leaving their relatives and homes to the mercy of the enemy in Finland.

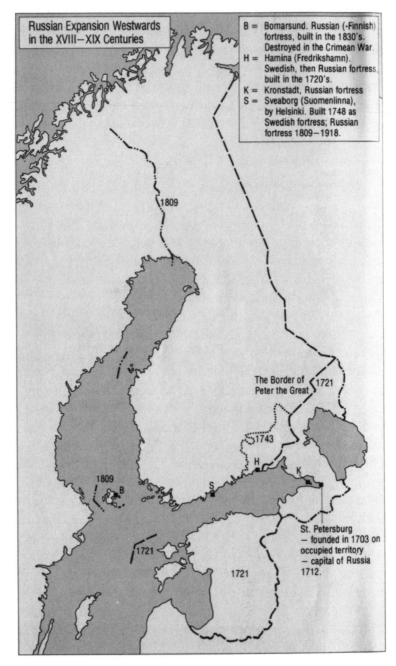

Reprinted from *A Brief History of Finland*, 9th ed., by Matti Klinge (Helsinki, Finland: Otava Publishing Co., 1992). Used by permission.

Introduction to Suomi (Finland)

As if wars were not enough, during the entire seventeenth century, Northern Europe was gripped by a cold weather cycle. Finland's agricultural belt was further north than that of other Baltic countries and suffered more crop damage than the others. The early frost of 1696 in particular ruined most crops, devastating the food supply. The Baltic Sea froze that winter for six months, cutting off supplies from countries south of the Baltic. Sweden was still able to ship grain from its southern provinces but spared none for Finland. People did not soon forget such treatment. Before the famine was over, about one-third of the Finnish population had died.

As Swedish power waned, Russian power grew enormously. Sweden fought two more wars against Russia, one in 1788-1790 in which the Finns played a starring role. On June 13, 1789, at Porrassalmi in Finland, the Finns were outnumbered seven to one by the Russians but still repulsed their massive attack.

Some years later, during the Napoleonic Wars, while Russia was waging war with Turkey, it still managed to concentrate troops on the coast of the Gulf of Finland, ostensibly to scare Gustavus IV, then King of Sweden. Sweden did not yield to the pressure, so on February 21, 1808, Russian troops crossed the lightly defended Finnish border. Finland's defense was left to her ill-equipped forces. For once the Finnish forces almost matched the Russians in numbers, but the Russians employed experienced fighting veterans from central Europe against the poorly trained Finns. In addition, they had unlimited reserves, while the Finns essentially had none. Sweden was afraid to come to Finland's aid for fear of invasion. As a result, Finland was overrun and annexed by Russia.

The Treaty of Paris (1814) ended the war and the victorious powers carved up the face of Europe. Sweden got Norway to compensate for the loss of Finland. The Tsar of Russia, Alexander I, took Finland as his private property, and it became known as the autonomous Grand Duchy of Finland.

Tsar Alexander I was a sovereign with a liberal bent. Under the Tsar, Finland was freer to manage its domestic affairs than she had been when united with Sweden. Consequently, Finland kept its Swedish legal system and governmental institutions, its religion, and its bank and currency, and had customs at the Russian border.

Finland enjoyed about 90 years of peace. Finns were exempt from military service in the Russian army yet enjoyed the protection of a major power. In Russia the peasants were serfs; in Finland there were no serfs.

Under the Tsar, Finnish industry developed and took advantage of a vast duty-free Russian market. In 1856 the extremely important Saimaa Canal opened; it connected the vast inland waterways of the lake district with the Gulf of Finland and nearby St. Petersburg. The tar and timber industries boomed, and the manufacture of ships and steam engines began.

The Tsar wanted the capital of Finland moved away from Sweden. Previously, Stockholm had been the capital of the united kingdom, with Turku on the west coast of Finland as its provincial center. The new capital, Helsinki, was built on the Gulf of Finland, nearer to St. Petersburg. The site chosen was a small village that had a natural harbor with a cluster of rocky offshore islands suitable for defense. The Tsar wanted the village rebuilt on a grand scale into a splendid city. It was to be a showpiece for the world.

Later in the nineteenth century, while still under Russian rule, Finnish nationalism exerted itself, and with it a search for roots and a national identity. Finnish had always been spoken by the vast majority of Finns. However, during Finland's association with Sweden over many centuries and with its administrative center in Sweden, Swedish gradually came into use in all government functions, judicial as well as administrative. Ultimately, to get a government position in Finland, Finns had to learn Swedish. Many Finns adopted Swedish names. Later, secondary schools were taught in Swedish although in primary grades Finnish was used. The situation became so lopsided that occasionally someone who could not speak Swedish was tried in his own country in a Swedish-speaking court. Such occurrences caused even more indignation.

After Russia took over Finland, the educated classes continued to speak Swedish. Hence, Swedish retained its former predominance, now with a further veneer of Russian. The farcical nature of this situation was not lost on even the well-educated Swedish-speaking Finns. A great groundswell of Finnish identity finally overrode the objections of the Swedophiles. In 1855, Tsar Alexander II ascended the imperial throne of Russia. Influenced by the liberalizing thoughts sweeping Europe, he was persuaded to recognize Finnish as the official language of Finland. In 1863 the Tsar signed the Language Decree, which recognized Finnish as an official administrative language. In gratitude, a statue of Alexander II was erected in Senate Square in Helsinki in 1884. Also, under Tsar Alexander II, Finnish autonomy achieved two important gains—a national army and a totally independent monetary system.

Finland had been regarded by Russian liberals as an ideal the rest of Russia could view as an example. However, the Russian nationalist movement called Pan-Slavism led to imperialism. As other European nations scrambled after colonies, Russia did so as well. In 1877-1878 it warred with Turkey in a move to take the Balkans and the strategically important Dardanelles. Turkey narrowly won the war with European help. This defeat frustrated and humiliated the nationalists, who psychologically aided the anarchists who wanted to get rid of the Tsar. The anarchists finally succeeded in assassinating Alexander II in March 1881.

Tsar Alexander III was made of sterner stuff than his father and did not worry too much about public reaction. His father had allowed the Finns a constitution that would have caused Finland to elect representatives to the imperial assembly, which would have enacted laws for the Grand Duchy. The new Tsar didn't act on his father's constitution because of the influence of his former tutor Pobjedonostev. Pobjedonostev, the powerful minister of education, wanted to retain autocratic rule in Russia, thus temporarily saving Finland from being absorbed into the Russian empire and losing its status as the Grand Duchy.

Later, a committee of Russians and Finns formed to create a new government for Finland. The Tsar delayed in signing the new code and died the following year (1893). When Nicholas II became Tsar in 1894, he swore an oath to retain intact the constitutional laws of Finland. The Finns naively believed their Grand Duchy status would be retained. However, the new Tsar instituted a policy of Russification as part of the previously mentioned Pan-Slavic movement sweeping Russia. Russian was made the official language of Finland, and its military forces were disbanded. Russians replaced most police and the heads of municipalities. Finnish officials who resisted orders were removed and replaced by Russians who spoke neither Finnish nor Swedish. Freedom of speech, assemblies, and associations were banned. Opposition was suppressed by imprisonment or exile to Siberia.

The notorious General Nikolai Bobrikov became Governor-General of Finland in 1899. He had previously made his strong autocratic anti-Finnish position known. The Manifesto of February 1899 placed all Finnish laws and the entire country under the control of the Russian government.

The Western world was stunned. A petition of protest signed by more than half a million people in Finland was taken to the Tsar in St. Petersburg by a delegation of 500 Finns. The Tsar refused to see them. Authors, scientists, and other notables from many countries also sent a petition that the Tsar refused to receive. A country that had been loyal to the Tsar now developed a bitter hatred for him, calling him the Great Perjurer.

Passive resistance developed. Peaceful demonstrations in Helsinki were broken up by Cossacks on horseback with whips. Schoolchildren refused to learn Russian. Finns refused to serve with Russian troops. And so on. Bobrikov is said to have asked a Finn how long it would be before the Finns spoke Russian. The reply was that Finland and Sweden had coexisted side-by-side for six-and-a-half centuries, and still only about 10 percent of Finns spoke Swedish.

During this period, Finnish nationalism expressed itself in literature and the music of Jean Sibelius and painters such as Akseli Gallen-Kalleta. Many of their themes were based on the national epic *The Kalevala*, the ancient folklore of the Finns.

Finally in 1904, as desperation grew, a courageous young Finnish patriot named Eugene Schauman assassinated the hated Russian tyrant Bobrikov. Schauman then shot himself. He became an instant martyr. The Russians were taken aback for a while, but Russification again intensified.

The socialist movement had gained strength in feudal Russia in the latter part of the nineteenth century, as it had elsewhere in Europe. The Russian defeat by Japan in the Russo-Japanese War of 1904-1905 (in which the Japanese were advised on Russian military matters by Finns) and the resulting social unrest gave the socialists what appeared to be a political opportunity. Workers in St. Petersburg and elsewhere went on strike. These strikes spread to Finland, frightening Nicholas II into repealing the detested February Manifesto of 1899. With this repeal, Finland's constitutional rights were restored.

In 1906, the Finnish Diet established a unicameral (single house) Parliament of 200 members elected by universal suffrage every four years. This form of government is still in place. The head of state was to be the President, and the head of government was to be the Prime Minister. Also in 1906, Finland became the first country in Europe to grant women the right to vote—well before the United States. (The Finnish language has no specific designation for male or female. This can be seen as an indication of the equality of and respect for the sexes.) At one stroke Finland became the most democratic country in Europe. However, the Tsar could still dissolve Parliament at will. He did just that, capriciously, four times in the first three years of the new government's existence.

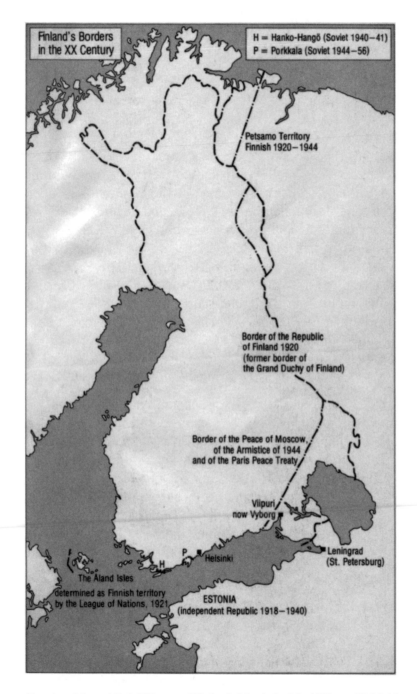

Reprinted from *A Brief History of Finland*, 9th ed., by Matti Klinge (Helsinki, Finland: Otava Publishing Co., 1992). Used by permission.

Introduction to Suomi (Finland)

World War I

Russification continued in spite of passive resistance. By 1914, when World War I broke out between the European powers, Finland was occupied by large Russian garrisons stationed at vital places across the country. These garrisons were holding down a population that was a powder keg ready to explode.

During the war, Russia suffered a series of devastating defeats on the battlefield at the hands of the Germans and their allies. Conditions at the front were so chaotic and deplorable that whole units deserted. The socialists again seized this second opportunity and overthrew Tsar Nicholas II and formed a new government, led by Aleksander Kerensky. As a result, the Finnish parliament declared itself the "supreme authority" of Finland because it was the Tsar, not Russia, that had a claim to the country. The Kerensky government denied this interpretation and dissolved the Finnish parliament.

At this critical moment, in November 1917, the Kerensky regime was overthrown by the Marxists (Bolsheviks). Their leader, Vladimir Lenin, had been in voluntary exile in Germany. Germany now helped Lenin return to Russia. Ironically, Lenin traveled to St. Petersburg through Finland.

Independence

The Finns also saw their opportunity to rid themselves of Russia and, with a majority over the socialists within the Finnish parliament, declared their independence from Russia. This declaration occurred on December 6, 1917, while Russian troops were holding a noisy meeting in front of the very same Senate building!

Finland's troubles were not over just because she was free. With World War I still raging and trade at a standstill, the country was paralyzed. There were acute food shortages, deadly strikes, and mass demonstrations. One-fifth of the population of about 3 million people were homeless.

The country's army had been disbanded by the Russians, and the police forces were weak. The situation was ready-made for exploitation by the communists, who had followed the example of their ideological brethren in Russia and had taken over many of the socialist elements in Finland. They also held control of many of the trade unions, especially in factory towns like Tampere—a hub of socialist activity.

The Finnish communists, in line with their philosophy of an armed struggle, formed a paramilitary organization known as the Red Guards, largely armed by the Russians. The democratically minded urban dwellers united with groups opposed to the communists: factory owners, land owners, and farmers (Finland was still 85 percent rural). They formed what eventually became known as the White Guards. The country poised on the brink of civil war.

Civil War

On January 24, 1918, with the threat of civil war hanging over their heads and after a bitter 18-hour debate, Parliament decided to organize an army. It was to have the immediate task of restoring civil order, disarming armed gangs, and ousting the 40,000 or so Russian troops still stationed in Finland. Russian naval vessels were also in Finnish ports. Russia was asked to remove her troops and other military forces from Finland, but she ignored the request.

Prime Minister Pehr Evind Svinhufvud, a plain-speaking, rugged Russian-hater, assigned the task of organizing an army to Lieutenant-General C. Gustaf Mannerheim and nationalized the White Guard. As has been noted in the past, great and able men seem to rise to meet the occasion. When the country sorely needed him, Carl Gustaf Mannerheim was there.

General Mannerheim and the "White" establishment realized that the "Red" strength lay in the south. The General and many senators and others quickly left Helsinki northwest by train for Vaasa on the coast of Ostrobothnia to establish army headquarters. There, the rural population of staunch farmers was pro-White, and the lines of communication to the outside world through Sweden were secure. Mannerheim was reinforced by the Jaegers—young men who had had military training in Germany.

On the night of January 27, 1918, the Reds staged a coup, taking over Helsinki, Tampere, and most of southern Finland and plunging the country into civil war. Interestingly, by sheer coincidence, General Mannerheim made his move at the same time as the Red coup to the south. His troops surrounded the Russian garrisons before dawn on January 28, 1918, and simultaneously took them with only slight skirmishes.

By April 5, Mannerheim's forces overran the city of Tampere. The Russian forces on the Karelian Isthmus were encircled and destroyed. By May 15, with German help, the entire Isthmus as far as the Russian border was taken, thus ending the civil war. On May 16th, General Mannerheim entered Helsinki at the head of his triumphant White troops. Whites in the south came out of hiding, and Parliament reassembled.

The civil war may have been over, but the war of liberation from Russia still continued. In May 1918 Svinhufvud was elected regent. The Prime Minister was J. K. Paasikivi. The new government appointed by him was packed with monarchists. Parliament convened without the 90 socialist members who had supported the Reds. At this point General Mannerheim resigned for reasons not fully understood. It may be because the monarchists tried to bring about a constitutional monarchy in Finland. Most Finns favored a republic.

World War II

However, before the monarchy came into being, World War I ended. Svinhufvud resigned two days later, and Parliament reassembled. It ratified a new constitution with Professor K. J. Stahlberg as the first president of the new republic. Finland was recognized by other countries, and the Peace Treaty of Tartu settled its borders with the Soviet Union. Finland gained Petsamo, an ice-free port, on the Arctic Ocean. East Karelia, populated by Finns, was lost. A comprehensive land redistribution program allowed every third family in Finland to own land. Education became compulsory. Legislation was passed guaranteeing freedom of speech, assembly, and religion. Finland accepted (and subsequently repaid) a loan of $10 million from the United States to ease the food shortage.

After independence, and between the World Wars, the country made spectacular progress in industry and agriculture. Political stability was somewhat regained, and by 1926 the socialists participated in elections, having shaken off the hardcore communists. Amid signs of a coming war in the 1930s, Finland hoped to remain neutral.

To the surprise of the West, Hitler and Stalin signed a nonaggression pact between Nazi Germany and the Soviet Union in 1939. These two major powers divided Eastern Europe and Scandinavia into spheres of influence between them. Finland fell into the Russian sphere, but the Finns refused to have Russian military forces on Finnish soil, citing their neutrality.

On November 13, 1939, negotiations broke down. About two weeks later, on November 30, the Red Army crossed the Finnish eastern frontier. Helsinki was bombed by the Soviet air force, and the Soviet navy threatened Finnish islands in the Baltic Sea. Because of Sweden's neutrality, Finland was isolated and cut off from help from Europe.

The Russian generals had assured Stalin that they would take Finland in one or two weeks. They were wrong. Even though the Finns had minimum training and were lightly armed, they knew the terrain and the forests. With the determination and will of a free people defending their home, they used ingenuity and guerrilla war tactics against miles-long columns of Russian tanks and troops. As a result, the columns were chopped into pieces that were then eliminated one by one. Mother Nature also came to the aid of the Finns in the form of an unusually cold winter, with temperatures dropping at times to -40 degrees F. The Russians could not build fires to keep warm, because of sniper fire and hit-and-run raids by small groups of camouflaged ski patrols.

Stalin sent an additional 600,000 troops and a huge number of cannons to the Karelian Isthmus. He also sent 2,500 planes against the Finns' total force of 300 planes. By February 11, 1940, the Finnish lines cracked, and by February 16 the Finns started a strategic withdrawal toward Viipuri, having expended most of their ammunition.

Finland sued for peace and surrendered on March 6, 1940. The Peace Treaty of Moscow was signed a week later. The peace terms were burdensome. Finland lost all of southern Karelia where 12 percent of the population lived. Almost half a million Karelians had to be evacuated and resettled in the rest of Finland. The country lost 10 percent of its overall territory, which included Lake Ladoga, a good fishery, as well as its second largest city, Viipuri. It also lost the economically important Saimaa Canal along with large timber resources and metal industries. Russia obtained a 30-year lease on the naval base in Hanko.

Many believed that the ultimate aim of the Russians was to absorb Finland. Russia interfered in the Finnish presidential elections, denouncing candidates it did not like and threatening Finland if they were elected. Finland was forced to agree to permitting military shipments from Leningrad to Hanko.

In what became known in Finland as the Continuation War, German troops massed in Lapland during June 1941. Hitler's armies attacked the Soviet Union on June 22. German bombers attacked Leningrad by flying along the south coast of Finland. The Soviets in turn bombed the southern cities of Finland. Finnish troops pushed into Soviet Karelia to strategic positions and then stopped their advance. They did not join in the siege of Leningrad.

A stalemate existed until June 1944, when the Soviets started their major offensive under the cover of an enormous artillery barrage. The President of Finland resigned on August 1, 1944, and was replaced by Mannerheim. Mannerheim and the Soviets held peace talks that brought about a cease fire on September 5. The armistice followed on September 19, 1944. Elsewhere, World War II continued.

The Winter War and the Continuation War had cost Finland dearly. Some 100,000 Finns were dead and 220,000 wounded, many seriously. The population at the time was only 3.7 million. Southern Karelia was lost a second time, with 420,000 Karelian refugees again fleeing the Russians. Finland's ice-free Arctic port of Petsamo and the nickel mines in the north were lost with other unfavorable adjustments of the mutual boundary. Finland's map, up to this point resembling a lady with upraised arms, lost an arm in this war.

The Russians demanded war reparations of $300 million in industrial goods, machinery, and ships within six years. Finland also had to surrender most of its merchant fleet. Many people doubted that it could be done. Entirely new industries had to be created to meet this war obligation. What irony, the aggressor wanting compensation!

Cold War

Probably to the chagrin of the Russian leadership, Finland emerged from all its hardships and devastation a stronger nation. Finland kept its freedom and avoided the crushing, demoralizing, and devastating effects of the Russian occupation of Eastern Europe. Kusti Paasikivi became President of Finland in 1946 and steered the country into a policy of strict neutrality and good relations with the Soviet Union. In 1952, Finland held the Olympic Games in Helsinki and Miss Finland was crowned Miss Universe. More significant, the last train-load of war reparations was sent to Russia that year, marking a major turn in Finland's fortunes.

Contemporary Times

The postwar years for Finland have been a period of healing, rebuilding, and consolidation. By 1985, through hard work, ingenuity, and frugality, Finland had achieved the eighth highest standard of living in the world. Economic ties with Western Europe have steadily increased, and Finland has now become a member of the European Economic Union. Rovaniemi, on the Arctic Circle, leveled by the Germans, is now a modern city. Its airport gets Concords flying in from England and Japan loaded with tourists who have come to see Santa Claus and the reindeer.

The most honored people in Finland, with few notable exceptions, tend to be its artists, playwrights, poets, folklorists, architects, athletes, and heroes. They are considered national treasures and the heart and soul of the Finnish nation.

History of Finns in the United States

Along with Swedish settlers, Finns came to America in 1638 to set up a trading post at what is now Wilmington, Delaware. They established Fort Christina, named in honor of Sweden's young queen. The first colonists arrived two years later. Some of these early colonists were young Finnish men who refused to fight any more of Sweden's foreign wars. Many of the Finns left the fort to establish communities such as Finland (between Marcus Hook and Chester, Pennsylvania).

The Finns were skilled craftsmen used to working with material from forests. They brought their home-country method of fitting and notching horizontally laid logs together in a pattern now known as the American log cabin—a warm, snug construct. This method is in contrast to the earlier, rather cold English cabins, which were widely spaced logs set up on end in the ground, using wattle in between the poles.

Our founding fathers were represented by Finns. One of the early settlers, Martti Marttinen, changed his name to Morton Mortonson; he was the great-grandfather of John Morton, who cast the deciding vote in favor of the Declaration of Independence. Many Finns in the backwoods learned the Indian dialects and served as interpreters during the Revolutionary War.

Finnish construction workers as well as Finnish sailors in Finnish-built ships came to Alaska by way of Siberia. After Russia sold Alaska to the United States in 1867, many Finns stayed on and drifted south to Seattle, Washington. Hard times in the old country resulted in 360,000 Finns immigrating to America between 1864 and 1920. The effects of the terrible famine of 1866-1868 (starving hundreds of thousands of people), combined with Finland's new industrialization, which changed the agrarian society to one dependent on commerce, pushed many to leave Finland. Other Finns came to escape conscription in the Tsar's army. Later, during the severe Russification period, political activists fled for their lives. Once in America, Finns headed for the areas where they had relatives or friends and that had a good possibility of finding work. Most of the men found work in mines, mills, factories, lumber camps, sawmills, and fishing grounds. Women became domestics. Michigan, Minnesota, and Wisconsin looked like the country the Finns had left behind, and they found work in the copper and iron-ore mining industries in those states. Montana and Colorado also attracted Finnish miners. Quincy Mining Company agents recruited miners in Finland to work in northern Michigan's Copper Country, bringing more Finns to the United States. However, many Finns became disenchanted with mining and bought farms, remembering the old proverb, "When one has his own place, he is his own boss." After clearing tree stumps, the Finns built their saunas, where they lived for a short while until the other buildings were built.

Wherever the Finns settle, they bring their own special quality of *sisu*. Finns can be especially proud of the contributions of their ancestors.

2

Culture and Traditions

Holidays

Independence Day

This is a national holiday celebrated on December 6. It commemorates Finland's Independence Day in 1917, three months after the armistice signed between Finland and Russia.

Christmas

In ancient times, the harvest festival celebration held in early November was transferred to December. The goat that led the pre-Christian harvest festival was transformed into a Christmas symbol. *Joulupukki* is the Finnish word for Father Christmas and literally translates to "Christmas goat." The old custom was for two young people to wear a ram's-wool hide with a ram's head attached to it. Another young person would lead this so-called goat. The leader, who was also dressed in a costume, would go about the neighborhood in the evening throwing small presents into each of the houses. Today the goat appears in straw goat figurines and mobiles made of straw that hang above the Christmas table or on the Christmas tree. Today, Joulupukki and, later, Father Christmas merge into the Santa Claus in residence at Rovaniemi, in Lapland, where he reigns in a special post office complete with elves and, of course, reindeer. Every year during the Christmas season Concord jets loaded with tourists from England and Japan fly there to see THE Santa Claus. Others come from all over Europe.

Joulupukki is the name for Father Christmas and is literally translated to Christmas goat. Straw goat figurines and mobiles made of straw are used in Christmas decorations.

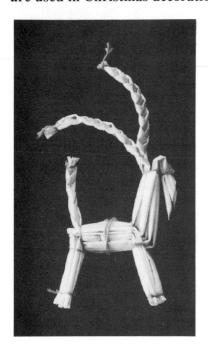

Pikkujoulu

Pikkujoulu translates to "Little Christmas" and originally fell on the night of the first Sunday of Advent, four Sundays before Christmas. Current Pikkujoulu parties are held the week before or after December 13.

New Year

For the New Year, a sauna party is a must (as it is on the eves of all holidays). After the sauna, people gather in the kitchen for coffee and *pulla* (a Finnish sweet coffee bread). Just before midnight, a small block of lead is melted and thrown into a bucket of cold water, where it immediately forms into a pattern. Someone reads the patterns and predicts the coming year's fortune. Bulging bubbles mean money, and black spots mean future sadness. If the lead forms a shape like a boat, travel is predicted.

Kalevala Day

February 28 is a day of celebration for the *Kalevala*, Finland's national literary treasure. This compilation in verse of folktales provides a contemporary link with the country's ancient mythology and is Finland's great literature of rural wisdom. The tales seek to explain the origin of the world and the elements central to man's existence: light and darkness, fertility, fire, death, and the plant and animal kingdoms. Heroes of the *Kalevala* bring order to a world of chaos through great feats and the intervention of magic.

Decorations made from wood shavings, straw, and woven strands of grain.

Vappu or May Day

May Day was a pagan festival to welcome the spring. It is marked by a carnival-like atmosphere with balloons, streamers, horns, and masks, and the wearing of new, light-colored spring clothing—even if it snows. There are concerts, fairs, and parties where special home-brewed drinks made of lemons and raisins are consumed. May Day is a time of putting the long, dark winter days behind and eagerly looking forward to the bright long days of summer in this land of the midnight sun.

Student Day

The evening before May Day, Finnish students celebrate Student Day. In the Market Square of Helsinki's south harbor, students wade through the water in the moat to the base of the statue of Havis Amanda, a sea nymph. They climb up to kiss her and place a student cap on her head. (At graduation from high school, students receive white caps with a black peak to symbolize their achievement. These caps are worn on other occasions.) Festivities continue through the next day with great partying.

Norma, Davin, Denise, and Emily, kantele players, at the Scandinavian Festival in Estes Park.

Jean Sibelius Festival

Every year in June, musicians come from all over the world for the Sibelius Festival in Helsinki. Jean Sibelius (1865-1957) is recognized throughout the world as a musical giant. He was inspired by nature and mythology, including the epic poetry of the *Kalevala*. His composition "Finlandia" was inspired by his homeland and is sacred music to the Finns. The song helped forge a nationalism in his country that made him hated by the Russians who intended to control Finland.

Kantele is the musical instrument created by the hero Vainamoinen in the epic *Kalevala*.

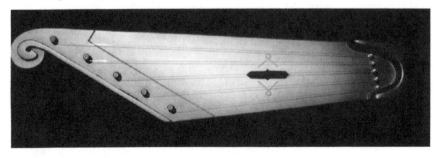

Juhannus or Midsummer Festival

On the evening of June 24, Finns go to the countryside to celebrate the longest, lightest day of the year. People decorate the outside of their homes with birch trees and branches. Bonfires are lit and people celebrate around them by singing, dancing, and feasting. In earlier days the bonfire was observed for revelations concerning the future; it was believed that spirits and ghosts made their own little fires to clean treasures. This summer solstice celebration also ensured good harvests, fertility, and magic.

Name Day

The name day, or the day of the saint whose name is shared by a person, is the day commonly observed in Finland in place of the birthday. Newborn babies are not given their names until a couple of months after their births.

St. Urho's Day

Finnish Americans have invented a tongue-in-cheek holiday such as the one celebrated by the Irish on St. Patrick's Day. Governors of the states have proclaimed March 16 as St. Urho's Day. Nile green and royal purple are the colors of the day. Thanks are offered to St. Urho for saving the grape crop of Finland from grasshoppers. That is why there are no grasshoppers in Finland today.

Music and Art

The Finns are great music lovers. Every year, particularly in summer, Finland is alive with the sights and sounds of music and arts festivals. Most are held outdoors and include the Savonlinna Opera Festival. The opera is held in Olavinlinna Castle in the Lakeland region. This castle, which is on an island, is an incredible setting for opera.

Finns have one of the highest literacy rates in the world, which is reflected in their love of books. Writers and scholars have been inspired by the folk oral literature as well as their worship of nature and their place in it. Their forests, fields, and lakes are sacred to them. The Finnish Literature Society was established in 1831, and the Folklore Archive contains almost 3 million manuscripts.

The work of a physician, Elias Lönnrot, in collecting the country's ancient mythology and great literature of rural wisdom from 1828 to 1844 into the epic *Kalevala* was important in forging Finnish independence. His work in recording the oral stories, songs, and poetry of the backwoods people of Karelia was part of the national movement to establish proof of an ancient culture that solidified an identity distinct from their Nordic neighbors and Russian rulers. Through his writing, the acceptance of Finnish as the official language of literature, as well as in education and government, was important to Finland's successful declaration of independence from Russia on December 6, 1917. Just as Jean Sibelius was influenced and inspired by the stories from the *Kalevala*, artists such as Akseli Gallen-Kallela have also been filled with the spirit of the *Kalevala*.

It has been stated by scholars that the *Kalevala* is one of a few true epics on Earth, alongside the Greek *Iliad* and the *Niebelungenlied* of the Germans, and gives reason to assume a unique knowledge not possessed by all peoples. The meter of the *Kalevala* is familiar to Americans because it was borrowed by Longfellow for his *Hiawatha*. This meter is common only to Balto-Finnic peoples.

Elias Lönnrot, the great collector of ancient Finnish folk poems, journalist, and publisher of the Finnish national epic, the *Kalevala*. Lönnrot was well known for his modesty and warm-hearted humor. This caricature shows him as a bare-footed country wanderer. The text reads: Unus homo nobis cursando restituit rem. (Otava Picture Archives)

Architecture

Finland gave the world renowned architects such as Eliel Saarinen and Eero Saarinen. In the United States, the St. Louis Arch and the TWA terminal at New York's Kennedy airport were some of the creations of Eero Saarinen. Again, the architects were inspired by nature. The best-known Finnish architect is Alvar Aalto. When World War II was winding down, the German army was driven from Finland, through Lapland and into Norway. The Germans engaged in a scorched-earth policy, destroying forests, villages, and cities. When the Lapland city of Rovaniemi was being rebuilt in the late 1940s, Aalto designed the streets of the city in the shape of a pair of reindeer antlers.

Art Deco style attracts attention with the Helsinki Railway Station, which reminds the viewer of an enormous radio from the 1930s. Eliel Saarinen won a prize for its design at the turn of the century.

Churches

Churches have demonstrated architecture in a variety of artistic forms throughout Finland. In Helsinki, the Rock Church is a spectacular example of modern architecture. For the church, the two designers, Timo and Tuomo Suomalainen, used a rocky outcrop that rises above street level. The interior walls were blasted from bedrock and spanned by a huge dome covered with copper wire.

At the other extreme of church building is the old wooden church of Keuruu, which was built in 1758. Painted murals within are detailed and delicate. The largest wooden church in the world is located at Kerimaki. The earliest church at Kerimaki was built in 1644, and the new church met the parishioners' insistence on a bigger church. Again, the interior is embellished with magnificent paintings. Neo-classical architecture is at the heart of the Lutheran Cathedral in Helsinki in Senate Square. There are also Orthodox churches whose architecture demonstrates the influence of the East.

Outside many of the older churches stands a wooden figure: the "poor man." Around his middle is an alms box for collecting funds for the poor of the parish.

Castles

The castle Olavinlinna, in Savonlinna, is the best-preserved stone fortification in Finland. Built on an island, it has three massive towers, double walls, and a useful amenity: On two of the towers are Northern Europe's oldest indoor lavatories, which hang out over the moat.

Although it is not a castle, Suomenlinna fortress in the Helsinki harbor was built on five connecting islands. It contained military bastions, barracks, and a naval yard and base. It can be reached by ferries, and today it is a recreational spot for strolling, picnicking, and historical study.

Olavinlinna castle.

Museums

In the city of Rovaniemi, the ultramodern Arktikum Museum is a multidisciplinary science center and a real adventure to visit. It was our good luck to first see this architectural gem rising out of the shoreline of the river as we traveled passed it in a Viking-style longboat.

Symbols

Another interesting observation from our travels in Finland is that symbols and emblems identify cities, towns, and tradesmen. These can be traced to a time before most people could read and write. Buildings and pictures were designed to be read like books. Everything stood for something else, and if you had the right "dictionary," you could read nature itself. Colors were significant as well in these symbols. One case in point is the Vaakuna, Finland's coat-of-arms. It dates back to 1581 and shows a raging gold lion clutching a sword in his armored paw on a red background (indicating a bloody battlefield). The lion is standing on the scimitar of the East, and it is thought that the nine silver roses surrounding the lion represent the original nine Finnish provinces.

Vaakuna.

Finnish Crafts

Glass and Ceramics

World-renowned, from the everyday to the deluxe, are popular internationally. Arabia ceramic ware is designed for functional use as well as one-of-a-kind art pieces. Iittala and Nuutajarvi glass objects are also world-famous.

Arabia annual plate with scene from the *Kalevala*. In this scene, Sampsa Pellervoinen cuts down the oak tree.

Jewelry

Designs include Kalevala Koru, which consists of reproductions based on prehistoric jewelry, the originals of which can be found in the National Museum of Finland. Another jewelry company is Aarikka, makers of distinctive Finnish wooden jewelry.

Fabrics

Merimekko is the most well-known of Finnish fabrics and apparel. Merimekko boutique fashions are famous for their bold design and bright colors.

Design based on Kalevala Koru design from grave goods of the Viking period.

Fishing

Lauri Rapala created the first wiggling lures for fishing. They looked like minnows. Fishermen used his lures with such success that *Life* magazine reported on the rapala lures in 1962. This led to millions of orders. To this day each lure is still tested in water and adjusted by hand, piece by piece.

Knives

The hunting knife, or *puukko*, is classic and popular with people who are active in the outdoors.

Puukko, or knife and sheath.

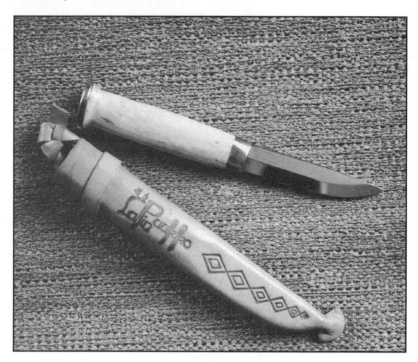

Woodworking

The forests are such a part of Finnish life that wood is used for all sorts of crafts and art. Furniture styles are distinctive. Traditional shoes, baskets, and serving plates are made from strips of birch bark. Schools for people interested in using wood in art forms include lessons in sculpting, inlaying, and home decoration. Wood shaving designs are traditional. Downtown Helsinki stores feature wooden toys and games. Classical saunas and their wooden buckets and benches are still in demand. A jack-candle is a piece of tree trunk with a lot of sap that has been trimmed and peeled. It is then sawed part way down its length, sometimes in the form of a cross. It is set on fire in the notch with birch bark on Christmas and New Year's Eve to light the way for the spirits. Smaller jack-candles (from one to two feet

---

long) are sold in shops for burning in fireplaces. With the cross cuts, the stump burns throughout the night.

Wall plaque at Teak, a woodworking school in Teuva.

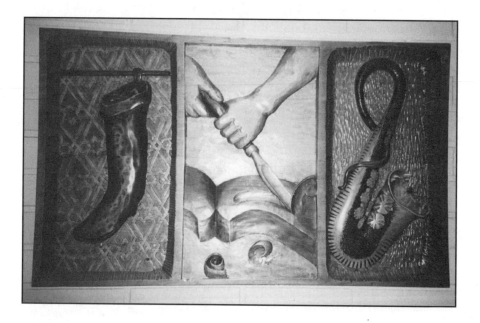

Rugs

Ryijy rugs are used as wall hangings. These rugs, which date from as early as the ninth century, are woven from wool and used as coverlets. In the late 1700s and early 1800s, *ryijy* rug-weaving became a folk art important enough to be passed down from one generation to another. Today, *ryijy* rugs are usually based on abstract or geometric patterns. Earlier pieces featured tree-of-life, tulip, or star motifs.

One of the design features we found interesting in all the homes we visited was the dish drains placed in cupboards directly above the sink. People hand-washed dishes and, after rinsing, placed them in the built-in racks to drip into the sink and be ready for the next time they were needed.

Ship Building

Finland has designed and built boats for many centuries and has produced many expert seamen. The clinker-built boat, where the external curved planks overlap, originated in the vast Finnish lake system and became the basis for the Viking ship. Today, Finland has become known for producing icebreakers (boats that break through frozen water) along with luxury liners, sailboats, and yachts. Ancient seafarer folklore holds that there should be at least one Finn on board a ship because he could supposedly calm storms or call up the wind at will.

Contributions

The Finns have been integrated into the communities of Canada and the United States and have contributed to the cultures of these countries in science, architecture, art, music, sports, drama, and manufacturing.

Log Houses

The Finnish log cabin allowed historians to track the original builders. To reiterate from chapter 1, their home-country method was to fit and notch horizontally laid logs together in a pattern. These cabins are now known as American log cabins.

Several of these early dwellings still stand. Near Wilmington, Antti Niilonpoika built one that is 300 years old according to records held by its present owners. The log and stone structure build by Martti Marttinen/Morton Mortonson is now maintained as a historic landmark of the Commonwealth of Pennsylvania. This homestead was built around 1655 and is a few miles south of Philadelphia.

Rail Fences

The Finnish rail fence was another important contribution of the Finns. They also demonstrate how Finns are naturally attuned to the forest. Some of these fences still exist.

The St. Louis Arch

Eero Saarinen from Kirkkonummi, Finland, created the "Gateway to the West" in St. Louis, Missouri. This gleaming arch allows tourists to ride up to its top and see the river and city as well as some Indian ruins from its majestic viewpoint. Saarinen designed many other famous buildings throughout the United States.

Literary Contributions

Another contribution of the Finns is to the legend of Paul Bunyan and his blue ox Babe. The Finns were the loggers and timbermen in Wisconsin where the stories of Paul Bunyan were created. They didn't have to stretch too far from the blue elk of Vainamoinen (the hero of the *Kalevala*) to Bunyan's blue ox! This is just another example of Finn influence. (The meter of the *Kalevela* is familiar to us since it was borrowed by Longfellow for *Hiawatha*.) In another literary contribution, J. R. R. Tolkien's *Lord of the Rings* trilogy bases the language of its elves on Finnish.

Sauna

One of the most remarkable cleansing rituals in the world is that of the Finnish sauna. It is a national mania. Both the body and spirit are invigorated and renewed. On a scale of one to ten, many think it is a twelve!

The Finnish word "sauna" refers to the Finnish traditional bath as well as to the bathhouse itself. Several Finnish folk sayings establish the importance of this national custom:

- If sauna, alcohol, and tar won't help, that's the end.
- Two places are holy—church and sauna.
- In the sauna, one should behave as in church—no swearing.
- Sauna is the poor man's drugstore.
- Sauna without a *vihta** is like food without salt.
- A madman has the sauna so hot that his skin comes off.

The wooden sauna structure itself, usually built near the shoreline of a lake, river, or sea, consists of a heat room with a fireplace covered with a pile of rocks that can be heated, generally with a wood fire (although gas or electricity are also used), and a dressing or cooling room. The dressing room is simply a small room with places to sit and possibly even lie down, with pegs for hanging clothes. The heat room is of unpainted wood, usually western red cedar, Engelmann spruce, sugar pine, cypress, aspen, or poplar. It has tiered shelves on which bathers sit or lie.

*"bundles of leafy twigs used to gently whisk the skin"

The rocks heated by the fire are generally rounded stones from lake shores and streams although some purists consider stones from the Baltic Sea the best of all. Larger stones are placed at the bottom, over the heat, with smaller fist-sized ones on top. Dippers of water are thrown on the super-heated stones, and it vaporizes explosively. The heat in the room reaches 200 to 250 degrees F. About 220 degrees is preferred by many.

Basking in the steam usually takes place at a somewhat higher elevation than the rocks. Bathers sit or lay on the shelves that are built against the walls. The higher a person goes on the shelves, the hotter it is. Refer to the carving of a sauna scene photograph.

The sauna needs to be well ventilated for safety and comfort. The equipment needed in the heat room is basic: a wooden-handled dipper and wooden or plastic buckets with water. Metal objects get too hot to touch. The floors in the heat room have removable wooden slats, and carpets in the dressing room are fiber mats or woven rugs.

For washing and rejuvenating, a sponge (*pesu sieni*) is favored along with the *vihta*. The *vihta* is made of leafy twigs of young white birch, about a foot and a half to two feet long. They are tied in bundles with the thick end forming a handle and are used to gently whisk the skin. This helps to set the hot air in motion as well as to stimulate body circulation. It also provides a wonderful fragrance.

Vihta are made up of twigs usually selected in spring and stored by hanging the whisks and letting them dry. During use, the whisk is wet or hydrated by being dipped into warm water. Old-timers will lay the whisk on the sauna stones and throw water on it to steam it.

Following several bouts of heating, washing, and cooling, some Finns choose to roll in the snow in the winter or take a dip in the nearby lake or river, which is a delightful experience. Some say that Finnish *sisu* (intestinal fortitude) is strengthened with sauna in the same way that steel is tempered by being plunged red-hot into cold water.

There are 700,000 or more private saunas in Finland today. That does not include saunas in hotels, health clubs, hospitals, apartment complexes, and factories. It has been estimated that there is a sauna for every five people in the country. Another telling fact of the importance of the sauna is that Finland is the only nation in the world with more saunas than cars.

A carving of a sauna scene.

The Sauna Society of Finland was established in 1937 to gather information and encourage research about the sauna. Most recent material concerns research studies regarding the physiological and medical effects of the sauna.

The sauna experience is for everyone, the average person as well as the rich, the young and the old. Having a sauna is a regular event as well as a tradition on the eve of every festival. Saunas are for cleanliness and relaxation and a very important part of Finnish life.

Part II

Folklore

3

Proverbs and Sayings

Proverbs, or moral sayings, provide a look into the value system of a people. Finns have a highly developed collection of these wise bits of advice.

- A bear thinks one way, its killer thinks another.
- What does an islander do in church? Sleeps and dreams about herring!
- Crazy is the fisherman who salts his catch already in the lake.
- The bull will live as long as we keep honing the knife.
- "Lords" are placed in front in church, in the back in a boat, and in the middle in Hell.
- That person circles the shore like a dog that's left on an island.
- As bright as a church's window on a holiday morning.
- Porridge keeps a man on the road. With gruel you get only as far as the gate.
- Better to have five cows with grain than six that are hungry.
- This horse doesn't need a whip, he obeys a stick.
- A pig plows much ground, but it doesn't drink beer on Christmas.
- When one has his own place, he is his own boss.
- A plank of flesh will not last—a bone log is slippery.
- Mother's advice to son: Do not judge girls by their best clothes, for on Sundays even a sow wears silk.
- War is a "pleasant disease" because it kills quickly.
- A man will marry a bad wife rather than none at all, as a starving pike will eat a frog.

- As unlikely to happen as this cock that is roasting on the fires of coals can crow, which it then does.
- While eating, if you dribble food or drink on the front of your clothes, say "Just visiting."
- You can get poor but you can't get thin.
- Violence gives rise to violence—and to law and order.
- In Finland taking it easy is a hard job.
- In wartime Finns said, "They ran out of intelligence so they handed out morale!"
- If you must fight, choose your adversary wisely.
- Stubbornness is a virtue if one is not stubborn about it.
- Laughter prolongs life.
- Love does not rust.
- A rooster is a poor man's clock.
- A debt paid is forgotten.
- Even the king's son is a child.
- Who promises much, gives little.
- Even a little bargain is a bargain.
- One castle cannot hold two kings.
- You sing the song of the one who owns the sleigh.
- He is master who rules himself.
- A full purse does not jingle.
- The weather hinders even war.
- A fish is beautiful in the water, but more beautiful in the pan.
- The crust is also bread.
- Even the most wise makes one mistake.
- Hurry slowly.
- It is still cake even if it is crumbs.
- During summer, one does not think of winter.
- No one dies twice.
- Sauna is the poor man's drugstore.
- Not every tree has a squirrel.
- Sleep is medicine to a child.
- Illness brings fame to the wealthy, but the poor never attain fame, not even in death.
- What one learns in youth, one knows in old age.

- A person with a long life lived as the pole of the world and as the pillar of the sky and kept the world from collapsing.
- An empty sack cannot stand alone.
- Do not lend your bicycle or your wife to anyone.
- Advice is good; help is better.
- It is sad to dance in another's shoes.
- Poverty and love are impossible to hide.
- When the copperware shines, the kitchen is beautiful.
- The floor serves as the child's chair.
- Better the bitter truth than a sweet lie.
- Better a small potato than an empty pot.
- Barking makes no wound if the dog can't bite.
- With money you can get, and with a horse you can go.

4

Folklore and Beliefs

General Weather

- ✠ Finns are wizards and witches who control wind, rain, and frost, according to their neighbors.
- ✠ Finns have had a special place in the mythology of seafarers. It was said that a sailing vessel should have at least one Finn, usually a sailmaker, for it was believed that he could calm storms or call up the wind at will.
- ✠ People in the Middle Ages spoke of Finns carrying the wind around in a bag or bringing a storm under control by tying three knots in a rope.
- ✠ A dominant motif in Finnish weather lore is a fear of frost, the sudden freeze that can destroy a year's work. (During the famine of 1697, early frost ruined most of the crops, and a third of the population died.)
- ✠ Frost is the son of the North Wind. He dwells in Pohjola, somewhere north beyond Lapland.
- ✠ Frost bites the leaves off the trees and the grass off the meadows. Frost freezes stones or peels the bark off the birch trees in the north. He comes roaring south with such power that he can freeze the milk in the ewe, the foal in the mare, the housewife's hand in the bread dough.
- ✠ If a cat sits looking out the window, it means rain is coming.
- ✠ Young cattle are nervous before bad weather.
- ✠ When you slaughter a pig and find it has a long spleen, the winter will be long too.

- If a dog pulls its feet up high while walking, a change in the weather is coming.
- Pigs carry straw into their sleeping places before cold weather comes. When warm weather comes, they carry the straw back out.
- If the magpie, the crow, and the hawk are quarreling, rainy weather is coming.
- When flies are eager to bite people, rain is coming.
- If waterfalls are roaring loudly, bad weather is coming.
- When bubbles are rising on the surface of the coffee and they hold together, good weather is coming. If the bubbles break up, weather you do not need is coming.
- In frosty weather, horses are lazy and just lie in their stalls.
- When goats come home from the field in the middle of the day, then rain is coming.
- If soot on the bottom of the pot burns, snowfall will come.
- When an old cow raises her head high and sniffs the air, soon a change to nasty weather will come.
- When the cows come home with hay pieces dropping out of their mouths, then rain will come.
- If a horse yawns, rain is coming.
- When one's ears are tickling, rain will come.
- If the cock is busy singing in the evening, it will rain the next day.
- Frogs croaking on dry ground means rain.
- If a cat sleeps with its head upside down, bad weather is coming.
- If fish are jumping high, a drizzle is coming.

Weather and the Calendar

- October 18 is the day the fox pisses on the birch trees (the day the leaves turn yellow in the autumn).
- The smooth days of January will be paid for in February and March.
- The sun at Christmas could mean frost at harvest time.
- The colder the winter, the warmer the summer.
- If one cuts firewood without a hat in April, he will work the fields in a fur coat in May.

- The Finnish year has eight seasons: spring, spring/summer, summer, summer/autumn, autumn, and the three stages of winter: autumn/winter (November and December), high winter (January and February), and winter/spring (March and April).
- May is "seed time," July is "hay time," October is "mud time," November is "dead time."
- May 18, the day of Eric: Cold Eric is a good sign; warm Eric, a bad one. Rain on Eric's day means a good year for hay. If you cannot hear the cuckoo on Eric's day, you will not find merry harvesters in the fall. Eric's day is the day to let the cattle out from their long winter in the cow shed.
- Rain on Easter Sunday brings a chilly summer. A sunny Easter means a good crop in the fall. For berry pickers, rain at Easter is good luck.
- If a cow's droppings are frozen in September, they will thaw in October.

Sami hat-of-the-four-winds.

- If the lanes are full of snow on February 2, so the bins will be full of corn in the autumn.
- If March does not show the ground, then neither will April.
- There will be as much rain in the summer as there is foggy weather in March.
- If the pig wallows in a puddle before the first of May, the summer will be cold.
- If it is raining on New Year's Day, it will rain when it is cutting and haymaking season.

General Proverbs

- If a raven caws in your tree branches three times, it means bad luck.
- You must ask permission of a tree before cutting it down.
- The dead wear hats and gloves of death.
- If a log sweats blood, strangers mean trouble.
- If a log oozes water, strangers are on a peaceful mission.
- If honey trickles from the log, there will be noble suitors.

Gods

Ancient Finns had shrines where they sacrificed grain, fish, and live animals to placate the gods.

Ukko is the god of thunder.

Ukko dressed in blue and pursued evil spirits and shot arrows at his enemies. These arrows fell to earth in the form of stones (meteorites?), and anyone who possessed these stones was especially protected.

Ukonsaari ("old man's island") is the island of the thunder god.

The rainbow is the sickle or bow of the thunder god, whose arrow is lightning.

Aarre is the treasure found at the end of the rainbow. It doesn't have to be gold, just something that is good for you.

Ahti was the god who gave fish. Considered the Neptune of primitive Finns, he had a trident, lived under the water, and was generally one of the good folk.

Wellamo was the wife of Ahti. Together they ruled in fresh or salt water.

Tapio was the god of the forest.

Mielikki was Tapio's wife and ruled with him as the goddess of the forest. They were good folk.

Pellervoinen was the god of agriculture. Because there were very few droughts in Finland, there was no rain god.

Vetehinen was like a ghost with long hair. She was a woman who sat on a rock surrounded by water in the lake. If you went in the deep water she would pull you under and drown you.

Ilmarinen was the god who ruled the weather. (*Ilma* means "air.")

Strange Creatures

Hiisi are aquatic and terrestrial creatures like beavers or water rats who love living in water. They make hissing sounds and have long tails with a tuft on the end, large eyes, a ragged fur coat, and a cap. They mainly scare people but are not aggressive, rather more like boogie men—parents scare their children with hiisi. They don't die. The hiisi live in caves, and their sex is unknown—neutral or "it." Children practice the phrase *vesi hiisi se sihisi hississa** for speaking skill and fun. The hiisi are also associated with metalworking and noise.

The nakki is an underwater creature. No one knows what it looks like, but it will pull children under water and drown them (similar to *La Llorona* in the southwest United States). The nakki is a troll who sits at the bottom of lakes and fishes for people, using the stem and flower of the water lily (the nakki-rose) as a lure. It is also said that the Nakki is a fiddle player or singer. He is fond of women and said to dislike clothes.

The tonttu is a shy, solitary, human-like male being, very bound to his ground. He can be very valuable for humans. In case of fire or other dangers, he can help humans by alarming or waking up the master of the house. It is very important to demonstrate appropriate respect for the tonttu.

Maahinen families live under houses or beneath stables. They like cleanliness, order, and warmth. They are said to move from a house if the house is abandoned by people. They might get angry if rainwater or sink water leaks into their dwelling.

---

*"*water troll hisses in the elevator*"—it is used for the rhyme and sound, not necessarily for the words.

Kaapio are social, asexual dwarfs. They live in mountains and mines. They are very fond of metals and beautiful stones and can get hostile when disturbed or robbed.

The metsanhaltija is a solitary female being of extreme beauty without a spine in her back. She mostly approaches hunters, probably to defend the animals or the wood from the suffering caused by human hands. The hunter falls in love and forgets his duties toward wife and family. He can also get lured astray or into a fog and die in the woods he thought he knew so well.

Keiju fairies are beautiful female beings, usually invisible but sometimes with visible veils. They are fond of pleasures and beauty. Sometimes they dance, sing or giggle. They are very often shy near humans. They dislike being disturbed but might fall in love with beautiful men and can then be very persistent. Open meadows, shallow tarns, and sheltered water mirrors can sometimes attract great parties of keiju.

Jattilainen are giants who live in caves, mountains, and deep woods. They are said to be insensitive to ice and snow.

Haamu are deceased people who live on after death. They have usually committed an evil deed in their lifetime. They cause illness, insanity, and death.

Heroes

The universe was plunged into darkness when a hero, usually a small person, came to deliver the sun, moon, and stars from the monster who had concealed them in his body. The hero then freed himself from the monster using various magic devices.

Peoples and Places of the World

The universe was held up by a *simsi*, a column or tree of life.

Pygmies live on the far horizon where the sky meets the Earth. These pygmies hunt birds with bows and arrows.

Manala, meaning "land beneath the earth," corresponded with *tuonela*, or "land of the dead."

Pohjola is the north land or Lapland.

The Tree of Life

The Great Oak is a favorite subject of ballads. The "Tree of Life" started as an acorn planted by four maidens, which gave rise to an immense oak. It was so huge and so tall that it concealed the sun and moon and prevented the clouds from flowing. Someone was sought to fell it. Many unsuccessful attempts were made until finally a man as tall as a thumb rose from the sea and felled the oak. It was conjectured that the Great Oak was a myth about the creation of the Milky Way. Seen from the ground, the Milky Way can be interpreted as a long, felled tree.

This "Tree of Life" is often pictured at the center of shamanistic drums. The original Sami (Lapland) religion was based on animism (a belief that all natural objects and living beings have souls or spirits) and shamanism (a belief in the power of a religious mediator.) The Sami shaman was a man skilled in communicating with the supernatural. He had the assistance of a magical drum. All family heads used these drums, but the shaman was considered most effective because he could go into a trance. While playing the drum, his soul would travel, with the aid of a helper, to the underworld where spirits could help him cure illness, make predictions, and avert disasters. The skin of the drum had many stick-figure drawings. To predict the future, a small piece of reindeer bone was placed on the head of the drum and the drum was shaken. The path that the piece of bone took and where it stopped was carefully read to reveal messages from the spirit world.

A figure representing the ancient god Ilmarinen from the shaman's drum of the hundred-year-old Lapp, Andreas Poulsen who, in 1682, was accused of witchcraft.

Afterlife Legends

A Sami legend of the northern lights explains that human beings are like the leaves that turn a beautiful yellow in the autumn because they are going to die. As death approaches, the souls of human beings turn brighter also. But while the leaves fall to the ground, the soul flies up to the sky. When the shadows of winter lie on the Earth, the souls come and show themselves to the living to give them courage to wait for the return of the spring and the sun. They dance from one end of the sky to the other, giving much better light than the moon or the stars.

The Finns and Their Culture

The sauna is the well-known bathing ritual enjoyed by Finns, with the three stages being perspire, wash, and cool off.

The enduring energy and proud spirit of the typical Finn is called *sisu*. A more common word for *sisu* is "guts" or "grit."

All country homes have an outside ladder to the roof readily available to put out chimney fires and for insurance purposes.

The symbol associated with the post office is a hunting horn.

Mailboxes are colored yellow.

The Lily of the Valley is the official flower of Finland.

Wedding Lore

As a wedding gift, the bridegroom gives his bride distaff heads used in spindle spinning, which are decorated and painted with red oxide.

In a wedding ritual, like a bridegroom, dance is brought in a bright sleigh (of many colors) on which birds are singing—probably bird-shaped sleigh-bells—until the whole house is dancing, even the stone oven.

Magical Objects

The magic *sampo* is a wondrous mill that was the source of bounty, a talisman comparable to the Holy Grail or another mill known as the *Grotta* that brings good fortune. It might also represent the sun and be part of the creation of the world and keeps the creation in force.

Sage and Medical Lore

A sage or wise man was literally a knower of secret lore, hence a magician, wizard or shaman.

In the ancient religion of the Finns, it was believed that an explanation of the origin of an illness would serve as a cure.

Sages always had a pouch full of various objects for a journey that were needed in addition to charms for different purposes. They might include flint, fish hooks, animal hairs, bird feathers, etc. One of the mythic Finnish heroes, Lemminkainen, needed only to take hairs or feathers, fish fins, human bones or hair, tree bark, substances indicating water and fire, and the like from his pouch. Then, by chanting, a bird, fish, human, tree, water, fire or other things came alive as was required.

Animals

Bears were once sacred throughout the northern hemisphere, and in some cultures they were too sacred even to be named. Hence, if the animal to be hunted was a bear, it was called "Beastie" in the rite that accompanied its dismembering.

The Finnish dragon is a *lohikaarme*, literally "salmon snake."

The cuckoo is regarded as a bird of good humor.

5

Folktales

Introduction

The history of folklore and folktale study in Finland is impressive and predates the establishment of Finland as an independent nation. The Finns are said to have the world's largest collection of folktales in manuscript form, most of which, of course, are in Finnish. For the highly literate Finns, folklore and folktales and folksongs are part and parcel of their national spirit, education, and pride.

The Folklore Archive of the Finnish Literature Society in Helsinki contains almost 3 million manuscripts. The Finnish Literature Society was established in 1831 and helped to finance physician Elias Lönnrot, who collected the folk poetry and songs that resulted in the publication of the initial version of the Finnish epic *Kalevala* ("Land of Heroes") in 1835.

It has been stated by scholars that the Finnish national epic is the third true epic on the Earth, alongside the Greek *Iliad* and the *Niebelungenlied* of the Germans, and it gives reason to assume a unique knowledge not possessed by all peoples.

The meter of the *Kalevala* is familiar to us since it was borrowed by Longfellow for his *Hiawatha.* This meter is known only to Balto-Finnic peoples. When runes, songs, poems, and tales become a national epic, they are often interpreted as the sacred history of a people. This epic is the source of that people's identity and strength and serves to transform both the creation of new myths and the passage of history.

The *Kalevala*'s essence lies in the shamanistic world-view. Its many heroes are mediators between the reality of this world and the levels of altered consciousness in the upper or nether realms of the universe. Shamanism is not a religion but an integral part of a particular world view. One prerequisite for the formation of a shamanistic world-view is a nonliterate culture, which existed at the time that the items that made up the *Kalevala* were collected. Lönnrot collected poems and songs directly from people who were still sharing them orally. As an epic, the *Kalevala* was created by a Finn in the Finnish language, and the Finnish people adopted it in a historical process as a cornerstone of its culture and its national identity.

With the publication of the *Kalevala*, the Finnish nation received a brilliant past whose existence had not previously been recognized. It influenced the country's culture in music, literature, and art. As well as Finnish folk songs, the music of Jean Sibelius was inspired by the stories in the *Kalevala*. Artists such as Akseli Gallen-Kallela illustrated scenes from the epic.

The stories of Finland are full of the wonder of the world, of existence, and of the transforming power of the human imagination. Elements of the natural world around them were also included as familiar details in the stories, poetry, and songs.

Finnish folk stories reflect a droll sense of humor along with a strong belief in magic, especially the magic of words. Ancient Finns believed in the existence of words, the utterance of which could accomplish anything. One built a house by uttering certain magical words. One made a horse out of bits of bark and old sticks over which one chanted certain magical words. Whole armies of men might be created in a moment by magical words. An explanation of the origin of an illness was believed to serve as a cure for that illness.

Along with words and magic, heroes explained the world. Heroes bring order to world chaos through great feats and the intervention of magic. To the modern reader, heroes should be seen as priests trained as warriors, poets, and healers who then are asked to take on large tasks on behalf of humankind.

Myths are coded messages from the ancient past. Spend a lot of time with a myth, symbolically add water, and watch it grow. As it gets bigger, we find out what the message is for our times. Myths seek to explain the origin of the world and the elements central to human existence: light and darkness, fertility, fire, death, and the plant and animal kingdoms.

The stories included in this collection, honed by oral telling over many years, were chosen to provide a varied sampling of tales from a unique people and place. Because stories travel, several stories are variations of others found throughout the world. Enjoy!

The Selfish Housewife

The venerable old storyteller (*sadunkertoja*) Erkki sat on a glacier-smoothed rock with the people of the village gathered around him. His grey beard wiggled as he talked in the cool midnight sun of summer.

"We Finns know that Finns are wizards and witches who control the wind, rain, and frost. We carry the wind around in a bag, and we can stop a storm by tying three knots in a rope.

"We Finns also know that Ukko, the god of thunder, lives over there on Ukonsaari, the old man's island. That is Ukko's island. When we see a rainbow, we are seeing Ukko's bow, and his arrows are lightning. He pursues evil spirits and shoots his lightning bolt arrows at his enemies. His arrows fall to earth in the form of meteorites, and anyone who finds these stones is especially protected.

"We Finns tell the story of the day the great god Ukko, all dressed in blue, went wandering among the *kataja*, or juniper, in Pohjola, or Lapland. He had been working hard chasing the evil spirits when he came upon an old woman baking bread. It smelled s-o-o-o-o-o good. The breezes carried the delicious smell to him.

"Even mighty Ukko gets hungry, so he followed his nose to the fresh bread, and disguised as an old man asked the old woman for a loaf of bread. She set about to knead the dough, shape it into a roll, and bake it. The whole time she did this, her mouth puckered up into a point. Her eyebrows were in a frown.

"When she was about to give the bread roll to the man in blue who had asked for it, she glanced at the roll and snatched it back. 'No! That is much too big for the likes of you. If I give you such a big roll you will tell others, and then every beggar that comes a-knocking at my oak door will expect the same. No, I'll bake you another roll half the size of this one.'

"So, she kneaded a second loaf and baked it. Her mouth puckered into a sharper point and she looked troubled. Once more she gave this bread a long look and cried, 'Why waste good flour on such a vagabond! One-half this size will surely fill *your* stomach just as well.'

"All of this made Ukko as angry as a steam kettle just before it blows. He spluttered and bubbled, and right then and there he turned the old woman into a woodpecker who spends its lifetime pecking, pecking, and pecking, and yet never finding enough to eat.

"With that, Ukko sat on the ground with his back nestled against the mighty oak tree, and watched the Northern Lights, which are really reflections off the shields of fallen warriors." ✠

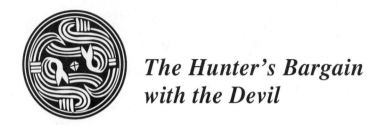

The Hunter's Bargain
with the Devil

There was a man, Johannes, who prided himself on his skills as a hunter. He had a wife and family who depended on him bringing home game for their food.

One day in the fall he went hunting and didn't come home with anything. The next day he again came home empty-handed. It was like that for many days. He traveled deeper into the forest but still wasn't able to find any animals or birds. If he didn't get enough game to feed his family over the winter, they would starve. He had no money to buy them anything.

"I have completely lost my good luck as a hunter," he told his wife.

As any good wife would do, she consoled him. "Don't despair. Things will be better."

Johannes was out in the forest the next day desperately looking for something to shoot and bring home. Now, he had heard it said that if one promises himself to the devil, the devil would help him. "If only the devil would come to my help so my hunting luck would change, I would promise myself to the devil," he thought.

No sooner had he finished thinking than the devil appeared before him. "Hunter, what were you thinking?" said the devil.

"I wasn't thinking of anything," answered Johannes, surprised to see the terrible devil before him.

"You were indeed thinking. I know you were thinking. Just tell me," insisted the devil.

"Indeed, I was thinking that since my hunting luck has been so bad that maybe you would help me," admitted Johannes. "I haven't brought food home for my family for a long time. Winter is coming and I am in desperate need. I was thinking to myself that you might help me since all else has failed."

The devil smiled. "If you make a deal with me, for three years your luck will change. For those three years you can go to the island in the nearby swamp. That will be all you have to do. You will just have to sit there and shoot, and I will drive the animals and birds to you. After three years I will have only one demand. You must shoot for me a bird that I have never seen before. If you are able to shoot such a bird, I will go on my way and that will be that. That is the deal."

"What if I don't shoot a bird that you have never seen before?" asked Johannes.

"Then you are mine and will come with me," the devil smirked.

"All right! That's good," agreed Johannes. Meanwhile he was thinking that maybe in three years he would be able to find such a bird. "Let's close the deal."

The devil took a piece of paper and said, "Drip some blood from your little finger on this paper. Also, make a mark on this tree with the blood. That will seal the deal." That is what happened, and the devil disappeared.

The next day Johannes went to the island the devil had pointed out to him. He didn't even have to stay there for the whole day. No matter which way he turned, he was able to shoot several birds and all sorts of forest animals. Every day Johannes went to the island, it was the same.

This went on for almost three years. He shot so much game that he became rich selling what his family wasn't able to use. He had enough money to buy whatever he needed. Life was good. However, he kept the source of his good hunting luck a secret from even his family. No longer did he have to farm or fish.

A couple of days before the three years was up he became agitated and nervous. He'd never seen a bird unfamiliar to the devil.

"What is the matter with you? Why are you acting like this?" his wife asked.

"It is nothing. Life is good. What could be wrong?" he answered.

But he continued to be nervous. It looked as if he would have to go with the devil and leave home. There was no way out of it for him. Finally he told his wife what had happened.

"I agreed with the devil that I would have three years of successful hunting. If I was able to shoot a bird that he had never seen before I would have won my freedom, but if I wasn't able to do that, I would have to go with him. Tomorrow the three years is up." moaned Johannes.

"So the only thing that will keep you here and win your deal with the devil is if you shoot a bird that he has never seen before?" mused his wife.

"It sounded so easy to me three years ago," replied Johannes.

"When do you have to show the devil this bird?" she asked.

"Tomorrow is the deadline," he said.

She laughed. "Well then, tomorrow morning you will cover me with tar and I will get into this feather basket and turn myself around and around and then I will certainly be a bird that he has never seen before." And that is exactly what they did. She was covered in tar in front, in back, and even on the bottom of her feet.

"It is impossible to tell whether you are a human being or what," Johannes marveled. "I'll make three holes to fool the devil into thinking they are bullet holes."

They went into the forest and there Johannes's wife told him, "You go over there and I will curl up here. When he comes and asks, just tell him that you have shot a bird that he has never seen before."

Just as Johannes got to the place in the forest his wife had pointed to, the devil appeared. "Did you shoot my bird? If you didn't, you have to go with me now," asked the devil.

"Just this morning I shot such a bird. There it is on the turf. Go and look," gloated Johannes. "You surely will not recognize it."

"Where is it?" demanded the devil.

Johannes pointed. "Over there."

When they got to where the feather-covered wife was, the devil looked at the bird, examined it, and went around it. "I recognize all the birds there are, but this is surely a bird that I do not know. How have you managed to kill such a big one?"

The devil examined the bird and found what he thought were three bullet holes. "You have won the deal, Johannes. I have lost, and I never expected to. Since you won, I will drive the birds and game to you on the same island for another three years."

The devil disappeared, and Johannes and his feathered wife went back home. They had quite a time of it getting her cleaned up. They had to heat the sauna several times and scrape and scrub her until she was clean.

For three more years Johannes brought game from the island, and they saved the money from selling it so they would have enough to last them the rest of their lives.

"I was right about the devil, Johannes. I knew he wouldn't recognize a bird that he had never seen before. He saw it for the first and last time," giggled the wife. Life was good and long for them.

The Magic Wish

Somewhere beyond the red sea, beyond the blue forest, beyond the glass mountain, and beyond the straw town where they sift water and pour sand, there was a woodcutter who lived in a log house with his wife at the foot of a gigantic oak tree. They had no children.

The woodcutter was humble and contented. He worked in his garden to grow a variety of vegetables. He grew rich wheat for their bread and tended fruit trees and bushes. He had a cow who kept them supplied with milk, cream, and yogurt. They grew fields of flax to make linen cloth, and his wife wove the soft wool from their sheep into clothing for them. Life was very satisfying.

One day a traveling peddler came to their home selling pots and pans. The wife bought several things from him that they needed and then he went on his way. After the peddler was gone, the woodcutter found an old book of tales lying in the dirt road. He took it home to his wife. That evening, she sat at her spinning wheel while he read some of the stories to her. There were all sorts of stories about magicians and changelings who granted people's wishes and changed woodcutters into kings.

That night the woodcutter couldn't sleep. All he could think about was magic and riches. In the morning he went quite dejectedly to work, which was very different from his usual sprightly self. He chopped wood for a while and then threw down his axe in despair. He plopped himself down on the stump of a tree and muttered that he wished that he could at least see a magical creature and maybe have a chance to talk it into granting him some wishes.

Suddenly, a bright-eyed rabbit seemed to appear from nowhere and sat looking at him while blinking one eye in a very knowing way. The woodcutter barely noticed the rabbit. He was quite concentrated on figuring out how he could change his fortune.

The rabbit asked, "Well, Mr. Woodcutter, what can I do for you? You have spent the whole night and most of today planning on how you can get yourself turned into someone special. I know a thing or two that might help you. For instance, I know where the wishing skin lies that the magicians have been weaving for three hundred years. It is now complete, and anyone wearing the wishing skin can have every wish fulfilled immediately. There is only one problem. As the skin is made of wishes, every time it grants one, it evaporates and the skin becomes that much smaller. If you are interested in it, it is under a lightning-struck birch tree. I have burrowed my hole there, and I will show it to you if you like."

With that, the rabbit hopped off and returned shortly dragging a large bundle behind it. He spread it out before the woodcutter's amazed eyes.

"Can it be true?" said the woodcutter. "Is this skin really made of wishes? Oh Mr. Rabbit, please let me put it on for just a few minutes. I would like to make just one wish and then I promise I will give it back to you."

The rabbit helped the woodcutter put the magic skin on. It fitted him somewhat tightly but was still quite comfortable. "Oh, how I wish this skin were mine," sighed the woodcutter. He had hardly uttered these words when he felt as if the skin fitted him just a bit tighter than before.

"Hey," said the rabbit, "What have you been wishing for? You look like you have grown smaller. Here now, give me the skin. I must put it back where I found it or I will be in great trouble with the magic ones."

Somehow the woodcutter knew he did not need to give up the magic skin, so he just looked at the rabbit and stalked off in the direction of his log home, thinking of great riches. The rabbit hopped after him, yelling. The woodcutter lost his temper with the rabbit and screamed at him, "I wish you would go to the north country and leave me alone!" The rabbit disappeared down the road and the woodcutter felt the skin tighten around him.

At home the woodcutter told his wife the exciting news. She asked him if he had been drinking and told him to go to bed and sleep it off. To convince her, the woodcutter said, "I wish there was a fine supper table filled with roast ducks, turkeys, chickens, pies, and puddings, and four servants to wait on us."

The table that appeared before them also had fruits and wines. The four servants were dressed in gold and silver. The husband and wife sat down and ate and drank and giggled. There was only one problem. The woodcutter felt a bit smaller. In fact, he was so small that his feet no longer reached the ground as he sat in his chair. He raised his glass of wine and exploded, "I wish to be a rich lord, I want a castle, I want lands and woods all of my own, I wish for velvet clothes, I want my wife to have silk dresses, our plates must be made of gold, our glasses should be cut from pure diamonds, I wish. . ."

His concerned wife stopped him because with every new wish he shrunk an inch before her eyes. There they were in a grand castle with marble pillars, soft carpets, and a great stone fireplace. Soft music filled the air. The woodcutter was only three feet high now, but he did look elegant in his new finery. His wife grabbed him up in her arms (which was easy now that he was so small) and danced them around the room to the music.

They were marched off to their bedchamber by their small army of servants. The next day they visited their extensive land, stables, farms, and dairies. Everyone bowed down to them and listened respectfully to everything they said.

The only problem was that the woodcutter felt that the servants were amused by his lack of stature.

That afternoon they rode in their gold-gilded coach, drawn by six snow-white horses, to call on their neighbors. Everyone around them lived in the same rich, glittery style. They returned home greatly disappointed and annoyed. After supper, the wife pointed out how some of the other women had diamonds all over their gowns, which was more jewels than she had, so she tried to talk her husband into making some more wishes. At first he refused but after his wife pleaded and begged for a long time, he wished that they were royalty.

Suddenly, everyone was calling them their Royal Highnesses, for they were now a duke and duchess, but the woodcutter was now only two feet tall. The lords and ladies took turns lifting him up into his chair and laughing at his jokes. Then the King and Queen came to visit them. That night at the reception the King laughed at the tiny duke, and the Queen made nasty remarks to the duchess about her funny little husband.

After the reception, the wife wished that she could be the greatest empress in the world. All night long they argued because the woodcutter did not want to shrink another foot. But he finally gave in. Before the sun rose the next morning, the woodcutter and his wife were now the most powerful rulers in all the world. At state dinners the husband now had to sit on a little golden chair placed on the table.

After a while his wife took very little notice of him and wouldn't allow him to have any voice in the affairs of state. She grew so uncomfortable with seeing her husband being carried around on a cushion that she had a tiny doll's house built in the garden for him. After that, she quite ignored him and seldom took him out.

Lonely and bored, he remembered the days when he had cut wood and slept the good sleep of the tired. He cursed the rabbit, the magical ones, and his own stupidity. Then, through one of the tiny windows of his doll's house, he saw a woodsman walking down the road with a bundle of wood, whistling a happy tune. The poor tiny fellow took off his crown and threw it on the ground. "Oh, how I wish I were a full-grown man, a woodcutter again, with my wife in our own cozy log house!"

No sooner had he spoken than everything around him vanished, and there he was in his own big ragged armchair with his feet once again touching the ground. His wife was knitting. They fell into each other's arms, and agreed that they were happier with things the way they should be, and they lived long and satisfying lives. ⊠

The Taiga Sampo
(The Magic Mill)

Vainamoinen, the oldest of the ancient wizards, was born of Ilmatar, the virgin maiden of the air, a spirit of nature who had come down to the open space. The winds blew her pregnant. It took 700 years for her to give birth to the seas from which she fashioned the Earth and all that is on it. She became known as the Mother of the Sea. Again the winds blew her pregnant, and for 30 years Vainamoinen grew inside her. His wisdom helped him find his way out, and he was born into the sea and waves. There he rolled among the billows for eight years. And so the eternal sage and stout-hearted singer began his adventures. One of these adventures was the creation of the Sampo.

Following one of his most harrowing encounters with a vengeful enemy, Joukahainen, who had shot Vainamoinen's blue elk, Vainamoinen was aided by an eagle. Not a big one and yet not a small one, the eagle was of a size in which one wing grazed the water and the other swept the heavens. Its tail was in the sea, and it whetted its beak on the cliffs.

The eagle found Vainamoinen weak and tired, for even ancient wizards lost their lusty youth. The eagle told Vainamoinen to climb on him because in the past, Vainamoinen had cleared the trees of Kaleva so the fields could be burned, plowed, and seeded to grow crops. In doing this he left one lonely birch tree as a resting place for the birds. The eagle had remembered this. And so, on the wing tip of the eagle, Vainamoinen traveled along the path of the cold spring wind to the North Farm. Louhi, Mistress of the North Country, took him to her home and fed the weakened hero. She presented him with a

feast of salmon and pork. She gave him a warm bath and rubbed life back into his muscles.

Vainamoinen was deeply depressed from his recent trials and tribulations and only wanted to be back in his own lands near his own sauna, listening to the songs of his own birds. He knew the North Farm was a place where other heroes told of people who ate each other and even drowned their own heroes.

"If you can forge a Sampo, beat out a lid of many colors from the tip of the shaft of a swan's feather, from the milk of a farrow cow, from a single barleycorn, from the fleece of a summer ewe, then I will give you my own daughter to marry and return you to your home," said Louhi.

Vainamoinen, weary and tired, told her, "I don't have the skill to do that, but my old brother Ilmarinen the craftsman can do it. He forged the heavens—beat out the firmament with such skill that there is no trace of a hammer or spot to show where his tongs gripped the heavens."

Louhi pledged, "I will give my daughter to whosoever forges me the Sampo. If you bring such a craftsman here, I will let you go to your home. You must keep this promise." Saying this, she harnessed a stallion to a huge sleigh and warned Vainamoinen, "Do not raise your head as you travel home or disaster and evil will overtake you."

As the sled traveled over the cold, frozen northland, Vainamoinen saw a dazzling maiden sitting on the edge of a rainbow weaving cloth of gold and silver and spinning threads of gold and silver with a golden spindle. Not thinking of Louhi's warning, Vainamoinen stopped and spoke to the maiden. "You most beautiful of women, come home with me and be my wife. I am the eternal singer. You will live graciously with me."

"Old singer of songs, I would only be a slave in your home as your wife. I would be like a dog in chains in another's house. No, I will not marry you," she merrily told him.

Steadfast Vainamoinen insisted, "I entreat you, while you remain at your home you are only a child. It is only when you marry that you will become a woman."

Being Louhi's daughter, with a cold gleam in her eyes, she replied, "If you can do some tasks, I might consider it. How much of a wizard are you? Tie a knot in this egg with an invisible knot and show me what kind of a man you are."

Vainamoinen knew that this was an easy thing to do. With his magic, he chanted and sang songs and sang vipers and snakes inside the egg to tie themselves in a knot. When this was done, the dazzling maiden gave the eternal sage more tasks. However, one of the tasks was almost his undoing. She told him to "Fashion a boat from bits of my distaff."

He sang songs of bravado and arrogance as he shaped the boat. He sang for three days. But as the boat was almost finished, his axe slipped and gouged into his knee. Blood poured from the wound in buckets and barrels. It stained the snow of the North Country. Vainamoinen started to speak the magic words of healing but forgot some important charms. In bloody anguish he got back into the sled and whipped the horse to speed so he could find someone who could heal wounds made by iron.

At the third house he stopped at, he found an old man who knew the magic to heal him. The old graybeard growled the charms to staunch the blood. "I am not familiar with the beginning, the origin of iron, where it came from. Without this information I cannot recite the charm."

Vainamoinen sang the origins of iron and its creation for him. With this information the old man recited the charms to heal a wound made by iron. When Vainamoinen was healed he said, "I warn you old man about the dangers of bravado and arrogance. I was guilty of using them as I sang songs to build a special boat. Never make the mistake I did."

Vainamoinen said farewell to the healer and got back into the sled. As he traveled home he knew he would have to trick Ilmarinen into forging the Sampo. As he drew near to the fields of Osmo, Vainamoinen sang up a

 bush-crowned birch tree. It was crowned with golden leaves that rose through the clouds to the heavens with its foliage spreading in all directions. He sang a moon to gleam in the gold-crowned tree and put the stars of the Great Bear in its branches. Satisfied that this would tempt Ilmarinen, he went straight to the smithy.

"Ho Vainamoinen. You have been gone a long time," Ilmarinen greeted him. "Where have you been and what mighty things have you done?"

Vainamoinen replied, "I have been staying in the gloomy North Farm skiing about on Lappish skis in the land of the north magicians. There are many amazing things to see there. If you can forge a Sampo with a lid of many colors you can win the comely maiden of the North Farm, daughter of Louhi. Many pursue her, but she will have none of them. With the Sampo, she would be yours."

Ilmarinen became suspicious. "Vainamoinen, old stout-hearted singer, I fear you have promised that I would create a Sampo as ransom for your freedom. Can this be?"

"Dear brother Ilmarinen, the things I tell you are true. The North Farm is full of marvels and I brought one of them back with me. Come see it." Saying this Vainamoinen led Ilmarinen to the tree crowned with golden leaves, the moon in the crown of the leaves, and the Great Bear sparkling on its branches.

"It truly is a marvel," agreed Ilmarinen.

"Look to the heights at the moon. Even you could climb up there and gather the moon in your arms as a prize," said Vainamoinen.

At this idea, Ilmarinen quickly threw off his blacksmith apron and started to climb the tree. "While I am up there I will get the Great Bear too." He climbed higher and higher into the gleaming tree and then Vainamoinen sang the winds to a fury to carry Ilmarinen to the North Farm. The winds carried the tree and Ilmarinen over the moon, under the sun, and on the shoulders of the Great Bear. They dropped him in one of Louhi's fields. Her dogs just stood there amazed. Louhi came outside to see what the winds were about and saw Ilmarinen.

"Come into my house," she said. "You must be the greatest of craftsmen I have heard about." As she came into the house with him she went upstairs and told her daughter to dress in her best gown made of gold, silver, and copper.

When the maiden of the North appeared in her incredible dress, Ilmarinen could not take his eyes off of her. She was lovelier than

Vainamoinen had told him. He must have her for his wife. And so he agreed to make the Sampo.

He had to build a forge and begin from the beginning. After he added the tip of the shaft of a swan's feather, the milk of a farrow cow, the tiny ear of barley, and the fleece of a summer ewe to the furnace, he saw things forming. But Louhi said of the gold, "These nuggets are just children's playthings." Of the silver objects she announced, "These are just a horse's jingling bells. Make me the Sampo."

And so for seven days he broke and returned to the furnace things that appeared until he finally saw the Sampo being born. He skillfully lifted it out and forged a grain mill on one side, a salt mill on a second, and a money mill on the third side. He formed a lid of many colors that spun around and held a bin of things to eat, a bin for things to sell, and a bin for household supplies.

Louhi was delighted. The North Country would never be poor or hungry again. She took the Sampo to a special place for safekeeping. It was placed inside a hill of rock, inside the copper mountain, behind nine doors with locks. It grew three roots nine fathoms deep. One root went into solid rock, a second into the sea shore, and the third into the earth near Louhi's house.

Ilmarinen smiled. "Now that the Sampo is done, I will take my beautiful bride and return to my own land."

"Ah wonderful creator of the Sampo," stated the daughter, "I do not have the time to leave here. The land and the birds need me. Besides, I am not ready to marry."

Ilmarinen could tell that there was no way to persuade her to change her mind. Downcast, he only wanted to go home. Louhi conjured a craft with a copper paddle. "This ship will be a gentler way to travel on the gales of the north wind than a tree was. Use it to make your way home."

Much time and many adventures and wives later, Vainamoinen and Ilmarinen were talking of how bad things were in their homeland now. Crops died. Coldness came and the people suffered. "While we are in bad times, the people living at the North Farm are in the midst of plenty because of the Sampo," complained Ilmarinen. "They have things to eat, sell, and store in their homes. There is plowing, sowing and all sorts of increase and everlasting good fortune in Pohja. All from the Sampo I made."

Vainamoinen decided that they needed to share the riches of the Sampo. "Let us go north and get part of the Sampo for our needs."

"That would be impossible," warned Ilmarinen. "The Sampo is in a hill of rock inside the copper mountain, behind nine doors with huge locks and with enormous roots."

Vainamoinen finally convinced Ilmarinen that it was the only thing they could do. So they set out by boat for the North Farm. When they got there they told Louhi that they needed to share the Sampo and the lid of many colors.

"The Sampo is mine alone," screamed Louhi. "It is mine!"

The eternal sage Vainamoinen said, "If you won't share with us, we will have to take it all." With that, he took out his *kantele*, a harp made from a pike's jawbone, and played and sang such marvelous music that the people of the North Farm fell asleep. While they were sleeping, he sang the nine solid doors open into the mountain of copper. Vainamoinen and Ilmarinen got Louhi's steer to plow and pull up the roots of the Sampo. They took the Sampo to their boat for the trip to the end of the foggy island at the tip of the misty headland to a space there unvisited by man.

However, a young, romantic, headstrong fellow who had traveled with them on this adventure started to sing a boastful song of victory. This reckless youth's raspy, roaring, quavering voice frightened a crane who flew off. The crane flew over Louhi's house squawking loudly and woke Louhi from her sleep.

Louhi discovered that the Sampo was missing. She beseeched the Spirit of the Mist to help her stop Vainamoinen and Ilmarinen. She evoked fog, gales, and a malevolent sea spirit to help her. The trials of the heroes were fought by Vainamoinen with magic songs of his own. The pike-bone harp was lost overboard in a storm, but that is another story.

Louhi conjured a warship with thousands of archers and men with spears. When Vainamoinen sang its ruin, she gathered the splinters of wood from the boat and made herself into an eagle. She flew to their ship but Vainamoinen defeated her again. With only the part of one talon left, Louhi seized the Sampo and threw it into the sea where it and the lid broke into pieces. With the Sampo sinking to the bottom of the sea, the waters would never again lack for treasures and of course, the grinding of the salt mill explains why the seas have salt.

In misery, Louhi set out for home. Her prestige was gone and she had been defeated, and that was why there was poverty at Pohja.

After Louhi was vanquished, Vainamoinen had Ilmarinen forge an iron rake with close-set teeth and a long handle so he could rake the billows to get his *kantele* back. With it he raked up water lilies, shore rubbish, bits of sedge, and the litter of rushes, but he could not find his pike-bone harp. But he was able to go ashore and gather pieces of the Sampo and its lid to take them to the tip of the misty headland at the end of the foggy island. With charms he was able to make them grow.

While he was doing this, Vainamoinen heard a curly-grained birch tree weeping and saw it shedding tears. He went to it and asked, "Why are you weeping, lovely birch? Why are you crying, green tree? Why are you lamenting, white-girdled one? No one is taking you to war. No one wants you for combat."

"I anguish because someone might peel my bark, pull my leafy branches off, slash me with knives, and use me for a berry basket!" spoke the tree. "Evil times of dark days are coming. Night chill and wind will take my leaves. I will be naked to shiver in the cold and to shriek in the frost."

"Do not weep, green tree! You will get abundant good fortune and a pleasanter new life. Soon you will rejoice in your new happiness." With that, old Vainamoinen fashioned the birch into an instrument. He carved out a kantele. He carved the body of the harp, the frame of the new source of joyous music, from the body of the tough birch. An oak was growing in the cattle yard, and he made harp pegs from the golden balls of acorns.

He made screws for the frame from the curly birch and then set out looking for something to use for strings.

He came upon a virgin sitting in the clearing who was singing to while away her afternoon in the hope that her suitor was coming. Vainamoinen went to her to beg for hairs.

> *Give me, virgin,*
> *Some of your hair,*
> *Some of your tresses,*
> *To be strings for a harp,*
> *To be the voice of immortal music.*

She did and so her hairs became the strings on the immortal instrument. When it was finished Vainamoinen seated himself on a solid rock and took the kantele in his hands. He adjusted the strings and regulated the tones. When he played the harp the curly birchwood sang out. It resounded, mountains echoed, boulders crashed, and all the crags shook. Rocks splashed into the billows, and gravel boiled in the water. Pine trees rejoiced and tree stumps jumped about on the heath. People marveled at the joyous music and stood with their cheeks on their hands. Tears flowed. Wild animals came to listen. Forest animals squatted on their claws, birds settled down on twigs, fish came to the shore, and even grubs in the ground moved up to the surface of the soil. Trees frolicked, flowers became sportive and joyful, and the young saplings bent over. He sang songs for good fortune for all times.

Many years and many adventures later, Vainamoinen prepared to depart forever. He bequeathed his kantele and his great songs as a heritage to the people of Finland. He got in his copper boat, and as he left, he blazed a trail, broke off tree tops, and showed the way for the new young singers.

Vainamoinen has gone. No one knows where he is or when he will return. His music has not been heard lately, but parts of his songs are remembered and sung even now. If you are worthy, you may one day hear them again. �֍

 *The Magic Millstone*

In the days when stones were turnips and kept growing and growing, and the sky was so low it had to be propped up with an old soup spoon, there lived two brothers, one of whom was poor and the other rich. With his neighbors the rich brother was friendly and ready to please, but with his own brother he acted as if he did not know him, for he feared that the other might come to him a-begging.

Not that the poor brother ever asked anything of the rich one—he never did. That is, unless he couldn't help it.

But once a holiday came along and the younger brother had nothing in the house and his wife said to him, "How are we going to celebrate the holiday? Go to your brother and borrow a little meat from him. He slaughtered a cow yesterday. I know because I saw him doing it."

The poor man did not like to go to his brother and he told his wife so, but there was nowhere else he could go for food. He dragged his feet in the road, kicking up dust as he went to the house of his rich brother and asked, "Lend me a little meat, brother. We have nothing in the house for the holiday."

His rich brother threw him a cow's hoof, crying, "Here, take it and go to Hiisi!"

The younger brother left his rich brother's house and he said to himself, "He has given the hoof not to me, but to Hiisi the Wood Goblin, so to Hiisi I had better take it." And he started off for the forest.

Whether he walked long in the forest or not, no one knows. By and by he met some woodcutters. "Where are you going?" asked the woodcutters.

"To Hiisi the Wood Goblin, to give him this cow's hoof," the poor man answered. "Can you tell me where I can find his hut?"

"Go straight ahead, never swerving from the road, and you'll come to it. But first, listen carefully to us. If Hiisi tries to repay you in silver for the cow's hoof, don't take it. If he tries to give you gold, don't take the gold either. Ask for his millstone and for nothing else."

"*Kiitos* (thank you)," said the poor man. "Thank you for your kind advice. Goodbye." The poor fellow went on, carefully carrying the cow's hoof.

Whether he walked long or not, nobody knows, but by and by he saw a hut. He knocked on the door and who answered his knock but Hiisi himself! Hiisi looked at the man and said, "People often promise to bring me gifts, but they rarely do. What is it that you have brought for me?"

"A cow's hoof," was the man's reply as he held out the cow's hoof to Hiisi.

"A cow's hoof?" declared Hiisi. "For thirty years I have eaten no meat," he cried. "Give me the hoof quickly. I am overjoyed." He snatched the hoof and gulped it down.

"Ah, now I should like to pay you for it," Hiisi said. "Do you want much for it? Here, take these two handfuls of silver."

"I don't want any silver," answered the poor man as he remembered the woodcutter's instructions.

Then Hiisi took out some gold chunks and offered the man two handfuls.

"I don't want any gold either," said the poor man.

"What do you want then?" bellowed Hiisi.

"Just your millstone," replied the man.

"Oh no, you can't have that. But I can give you as much money as you like," snarled Hiisi.

The poor man would not agree and kept asking for the millstone just as the woodcutters had told him to do.

"I have eaten the cow's hoof," Hiisi said, "and I suppose I will have to pay you for it. So be it! Take my millstone, but do you know what to do with it?"

"No, I don't," answered the poor man. "Will you tell me what to do?"

"Well," said Hiisi. "This is no simple millstone. It will give you whatever you tell it to give you. You only need to say, 'Grind, my millstone!' If you want it to stop, just say, 'Enough and have done!' and the millstone will stop. Now, be off with you. You have driven a hard deal."

"*Kiitos*!" said the poor man to Hiisi. He set off homewards with his millstone. For a long time he walked in the forest. He walked until it grew dark. Then rain fell in torrents. The wind whistled, and the branches of trees struck him in the face and on his shoulders. It was morning by the time the poor man came home.

"Where have you been wandering all day and all night?" asked his wife. "I was beginning to think that I might never see you again."

"You'll never guess where I was! I was at the house of Hiisi the Wood Goblin himself," blurted the poor man. "See what he has given me." With that, he took the millstone out of his bag.

"Grind, my millstone!" he told it. "Give us nice things to eat for the holiday."

The millstone began to turn round and round of itself. Flour, grain, sugar, meat, fish, and everything else one could wish for poured onto the table. The poor man's wife brought sacks and bowls, and she filled them full of food.

The poor man tapped the millstone with his finger and said, "Enough and have done!" and the millstone stopped grinding at once and came to a standstill.

The poor man's family had as good a holiday as anyone in the village. Their life from that time changed for the better. There was enough and to spare in the house, so the wife and children had fine new clothes and shoes. They wanted for nothing.

Sami slippers of reindeer fur and felt trim.

One day the poor man ordered his millstone to grind him a good measure of oats for his horse. The millstone did so. The horse ate the oats as he stood by the house.

Just then, the rich brother sent his workman to the lake to water his horses. The workman drove the horses to the lake, but as they were passing the poor brother's house they stopped and began eating oats alongside the poor man's horse.

The rich brother saw them from his house, and he came out onto his porch. "Hey there!" he called to the workman. "Lead the horses away at once! They are picking up sweepings and they will get sick!"

The workman brought back the horses. "You were wrong, master," he said. "Those were not sweepings but the choicest oats I have ever seen. Your brother has oats and everything else in abundance."

This aroused the rich brother's curiosity. "I think I will go and see how such a miracle could have possibly come to pass. How has my brother suddenly become rich?"

He went over to his brother's house to see for himself. "How have you become rich all of a sudden?" he asked his brother. "Where did all these good things I see come from?"

The poor brother told him honestly, "Hiisi helped me."

"What do you mean?" the rich brother asked.

"Exactly what I said. You gave me a cow's hoof on the eve of the holiday and told me to go to Hiisi with it. That is just what I did. I gave Hiisi the hoof, and in return, he made me a present of a magic millstone. It is this millstone that gives me everything I ask for."

"Show me this magic millstone," demanded his brother.

"As you wish," said the poor brother. He ordered the millstone to give them delicacies of all sorts to eat. The millstone at once began turning, and it loaded the table with *piirakkaa*, smoked salmon, cakes, roasted meats, and lots of other good things.

The rich brother just stood there with his eyes and mouth wide open. "Sell me the millstone," he begged his brother.

"Oh no," answered the poor brother. "I need it myself."

But the rich brother wouldn't take "no" for an answer. "Name your price, only sell it to me!" he urged.

"I told you it is not for sale," the poor man repeated.

The rich brother realized he would not gain anything by badgering his brother, so he tried a different approach. "Was there ever anyone as ungrateful as you!" he cried. "Who gave you the cow's hoof in the first place?"

"It was you of course," answered the poor brother.

"There you are then! You begrudge me the millstone." wheedled the rich brother. "Well, if you won't sell it to me, at least lend it to me for a while."

The poor brother thought over this request. "Have it your own way," he finally said. "You can borrow it for a spell."

The rich brother was delighted. He seized the millstone and ran home with it, without ever thinking as to what was required to make it stop turning.

The very next morning he put out to sea in a boat, taking the millstone with him. "Everyone is salting fish right now," he thought to himself. "Salt is expensive so I will trade in salt and get rich." He was well out to sea by now so he told the millstone, "Grind, my millstone! I need salt, and the more the better."

The millstone started spinning and turning, and the purest whitest salt poured from it. The rich man looked on in glee, rubbing his hands together as he calculated how rich he would become. It was high time to tell the millstone to stop, but all he did was to repeat from time to time, "Grind my millstone, grind, don't stop."

The salt began to get so deep and heavy that the boat settled deeper and deeper in the water. The rich brother seemed to have taken leave of his senses, for he did nothing but repeat the words, "Grind my millstone, grind!"

By now the water was gushing over the sides of the boat and sloshing over the salt. The boat was near to sinking and the older brother suddenly came to his senses. "Stop grinding, millstone," he shouted.

But the millstone went on grinding as before.

"Stop grinding, millstone! Stop grinding right now, I say!" the rich man shouted again.

The millstone went right on grinding unceasingly. The rich brother tried to snatch up the millstone and throw it overboard but it seemed to have grown fast to the deck, for he could not budge it.

"Help!" screamed the rich brother. "Save me! Help!" But there was no one there to save him and no one there to help him. The boat sank, taking the rich brother with it into the watery deep and the sea closed over him, the boat, and the millstone.

Whatever happened to the millstone? They say that even at the bottom of the sea it never stopped grinding and it just makes more and more and more salt. That, believe it or not, is why sea water is salty! ✠

The Magic Fish of Gold

There was once, I don't know where, beyond seven times seven countries, and at a cock's crow even beyond them, an immense, tall, quivering birch tree. It grew along seven times seven lakes that had seven times seventy-seven islands on them. This tree had seven times seventy-seven branches. On each branch there were seven times seventy-seven crows' nests, and in each nest seven times seventy-seven young crows. It was in such a place that this story belongs.

There was once an old fisherman and his wife who lived by the shore of a clear blue lake in a small house made of logs. He had fished in the lakes around them for more than seven times seven years. She grew flax and wove cloth from the flax. She also raised some sheep that she used for their wool. Between the two of them, they ate well and were warmly dressed, and that was that.

One morning, the fishing was very poor. The old fisherman had caught nothing, but he decided to cast out his net one more time. This time when he gathered in his net he had one fish. Not just an ordinary fish, but one that was made of pure gold. Its fins were gold. Its scales, eyes, and tail were gold.

"Ah well, this special fish is better than nothing," he said to himself and opened his birch bark fish basket to put it in for the trip back home. "My wife will find pleasure in this beautiful fish."

Just as he started to drop the gold fish into his basket it began to implore him, "Put me back into the lake, old fisherman. If you do, I'll give you whatever you ask me! I'll reward you richly."

The old fisherman stroked his grey beard, and being a kind, gentle man, he carefully slid the fish back into the lake. "Enjoy, little fish. Go back where you belong."

When he returned home his wife took his fish basket and looked in to see what he had caught that day. There was nothing in the basket. "How can this be? There are no fish for supper in here!" she grumbled.

"I was able to catch only one fish today, but it was a special one. It was pure gold and it talked. It promised to reward me richly if I returned it to the lake, so I took pity on it and let it swim free," he told her.

"What? You mean that you let such a wonderful fish escape? Why didn't you ask it for a house that has a roof without leaks?" she scolded him.

He didn't like it when his wife was cross with him, so he went back to the shore of the lake. "Golden fish, golden fish," he called out.

He saw the fish swim right up to the beach in front of him. "Why did you call me?" asked the fish.

"My wife wants a house that has a roof without leaks." explained the old fisherman. "Can you help us?"

"Go home. It is done," said the fish before it turned and disappeared into the lake.

When he got back home, lo and behold! Their log house had a new roof with sturdy beams and thick thatch on it.

Instead of being pleased, his wife scolded him even louder. "If the fish can do this, why don't you ask it for a fine new house with a separate room to sleep in?"

The old fisherman knew there would be no peace that night unless he did as she asked. He went back to the lake and called, "Golden fish, golden fish, I need you."

Just as before, the fish swam into the shallow water near the old man's feet. "You have called me. What do you want from me?" asked the fish.

"Forgive me, you amazing fish. I thank you for the new roof on our cabin, but now my wife wants a fine new house with a separate room to sleep in." the old man told him.

"Go home. It is done," said the fish and it turned, flipped its tail, and was off into the lake.

When he went back home he wasn't sure if he had taken a wrong turn, because where his log cabin used to be sat a beautiful red-painted house, with shutters, a porch, and curtains. Inside was a big kitchen with a large fireplace with a big chimney that had room in the back for a person to rest and get warm. There were fine curtains, rugs, and, just as he had asked, a separate room to sleep in.

But his wife still wasn't satisfied. "You have no imagination husband!" she shouted at him. "Why didn't you ask the fish for a castle? I don't want to be a peasant all my life! I want to be a fine lady with fancy clothes and jewelry. Why shouldn't we have a carriage with horses too? I'm furious that you didn't think to ask for this." She threw a plate at him for emphasis. Luckily, he ducked, and the plate smashed into the wall of the new house and flew into many pieces.

So, back to the shore of the lake he went. Would his wife never be happy? "Golden fish, golden fish, I really need your help."

With a ripple and a splash, the fish swam to the shore. "What is it old fisherman? Why do you call me?"

The old man explained, "Please excuse me, dear fish, but my wife is crankier than I have ever seen her. She even threw a dish at me. Please excuse me, but I do need your help. Now she wants a castle, fine clothes, jewelry, a carriage, and horses. What am I to do?"

"Go home. It is all as you have asked," announced the fish as it jumped back into the lake.

Sure enough, when the old man got back to where his cabin had first been, then the house that replaced it, he found a fancy castle with several stories. He could see special places on the upper-story outside walls where he and his wife could have their own indoor facilities for toilet needs. He found his wife inside the castle sitting at a long wooden table in an elaborate padded chair carved with faces of animals.

"I hope that you are happy now," he said. "What more could people such as us want?" He was sure that this was all that anyone could want.

The windows even had glass in them to let in the light yet keep out the winds. The golden fish had given them riches beyond dreams.

Weeks went by, and his wife tried on all her new clothes, went for rides in her carriage, and got more and more impatient. Then, as if she could hold it no longer, she exploded. "Is this the best that the fish can give us? As I ride around I see other people with great armies. I want bands that will constantly play music for us. I want stables of horses. I want the finest amber jewelry that there is. I want grand boats that travel around the lakes so everyone can see that I am of highest royalty." Her shrill shrieks could be heard throughout the castle.

As the old man walked back to the shore of the lake he wondered how it all could have come to this. Was there no pleasing her? Where would her greed get them? But wearily he called out, "Golden fish, golden fish. Do not be angry, but my wife has sent me back to ask for yet more."

With a swish and a splash the fish appeared. "What is it this time, old man? What more could this wife of yours want?"

The old fisherman told the fish the latest demands. The fish stood on its tail, twirled around, and said, "Go home, it is done," as it dashed back out to the lake.

Sure enough, before he even got home, he saw a huge boat loaded with people having a party out on the lake. A band played music on the boat. There was more. The old man had to make his way through enormous armies to get into the castle. There sat his wife listening to a band playing marches and dance music. His wife was covered with amber necklaces, bracelets, rings, and earrings and had amber beads hanging from her gown. Truly the fish had done all that was asked and more.

But again, this wasn't to be the end of it. His wife threw golden goblets at him and demanded that she become the mighty ruler of the lakes and rule over the golden fish. She wanted her castle to be in the middle of the lake rising to the sky. She demanded the power to raise storms that would strike terror into the hearts of people and beasts that beheld it. "You go tell the golden fish what I want!" she screamed. She was so furious that he didn't dare refuse her wishes.

At the shore, the trembling old fisherman became aware of a great storm raging in the lake. Waters billowed and roiled over the shore. Clouds burst forth walls of water. But still he called out, "Golden fish, golden fish. Hear my cry for help!"

Out of the storm appeared the golden fish. This time the fish was clearly angry. "What more could this woman possibly want? Has she no shame? What is it this time?"

The soggy, beaten old fisherman told the golden fish of his wife's new demands. "Forgive me, golden fish—" he said as he bowed his head.

Before the old man could finish what he was saying, the golden fish only turned around and slapped his tail on the water and slid back out into the deep.

When the old fisherman returned home, there was his old log cabin with the roof that leaked. On the doorstep sat his old wife dressed in her old patched and tattered clothes!

 *Timo the Musician*

In days gone by, there lived a poor, landless peasant who was more generously blessed with children than with food. His children had to learn early to help their father support this large family. Of his many children, only one son was lazy. The village people described him as having some idler's blood under his nails.

Nothing worked, whether it was patience or punishment. The boy just grew lazier and lazier as time went on. You knew where he would be in the winter—just behind the stove. He spent his summers resting in the shade of blossoming berry bushes, and his only work was to whistle and play tunes on his willow-pipe. Everyone who heard him agreed that this boy did very well indeed.

One summer day, as he sat under a bush alongside the road, he seemed to be dueling with the birds in the art of whistling. An old traveler with a gray beard called out to him in a friendly way, "Hello there! What trade do you prefer?"

"None at all. Nothing interests me. So that I should never need to work and to obey the orders of other people, all I need is to be a rich man."

"Now there is the problem. How can you become rich if you do not work? No mouse runs into the mouth of a sleeping cat. Anyone who wants to be rich must earn it with diligence and work."

The boy interrupted him impatiently, "Stop. No more! I have heard this hundreds of times from my family, but all of these words are just like water running off a duck's back. I will never become someone else's hands and feet."

The old traveler then suggested that the boy should make use of his gift with music and make that his trade. "Get yourself some instrument, learn to play it as cleverly as you play your willow-pipe, and you will earn food and money wherever people live who want to be entertained."

This sounded like a good idea to the lazy boy, but he still had a problem. "That is all very good, but how can I earn the money to buy an instrument?"

The old man smiled. "Play your willow-pipe, whistle, and sing for some money. You are already perfect at doing this. With the money you get you can buy yourself an instrument. Someday I'll be by this way again, and I hope to see you and what you have accomplished." With that, the old traveler went on his way down the dirt road.

Timo—that was the boy's name—was pleased with the whole idea and decided to follow the old man's advice and seek his fortune. He left home without saying a word to anyone about what he planned to do. Actually, his parents were glad to be rid of this lazy son. His father hoped that Timo would lose his idle ways and become a different kind of man as he ventured into the wide world.

For weeks, Timo strolled from farm to farm, from manor to manor, from village to village. The people he met were kind to him and they all seemed to enjoy his music. He earned enough to eat and drink with sometimes some money left over. This money Timo hoarded very carefully until he had enough to buy a good violin. He worked at learning to play it and in a few years he became a famous fiddler. No feasts, weddings, or celebrations were held without Timo the Violinist. It was almost as if he was a famous magician; everyone from far and near knew his name. The rich and the poor alike admired his playing and competed with each other to have him play at their events. Timo received many generous gifts, and beautiful young maidens tied silk ribbons to his hat. Ladies knitted him colorful gloves in complicated patterns.

Timo was well on his way to becoming a rich man. There was only one problem—he did not appreciate his good fortune. His greed grew and drove him on to new wanderings. In his childhood he had heard glorious tales about the opulent wealth of the lands to the east. He felt he could easily make the fortune he desired if he could only get there.

With that in mind, he roamed along the seashore hoping to find a ship that would take him across the sea to the land of his desires. He came upon a harbor city with many foreign boats docked there. After questioning the seamen he found a ship that was headed to the lands to the east. Because he was such a stingy fellow, he felt the fare for passage on the ship was higher than he wanted to pay. He smuggled himself on board the ship and hid in a dark corner among some barrels. One of the sailors helped him hide there for some money.

The ship traveled out into the open sea, and Timo's friend signaled for him to come out. The sailor was alone on the deck, on watch for the night. He told Timo to pretend to be drowning so he could be rescued and then be taken on board the ship legally. The sailor tied a strong rope around Timo's waist, fastened the other end of the rope to the ship rail, and lowered Timo into the sea. Timo was worried about this, but he knew he was a good swimmer and was sure he could keep himself on the surface of the water for a while.

When he was in the water, the sailor awoke the crew with loud shouts and called them to come look at what he saw swimming in the wake of the ship. Everyone was astonished. When the Captain came he called out to Timo, "Are you a ghost or a mortal being?"

Timo yelled back, "I am a poor mortal whose strength is running out. I will die if you don't take pity on me."

The Captain ordered a rope to be thrown out to Timo and to pull him out. Timo grabbed the end of the rope, while at the same time he cut off the other rope he already had tied around him.

When he was "saved" and on board the ship the Captain asked Timo, "How did you get here?"

"I did not have money for passage to the rich lands to the east so I swam behind your boat all the way from the harbor." gasped Timo.

The Captain ordered dry clothes for Timo and told him, "You should be grateful that you are alive. This boat is headed east. We will all get there together."

Timo retrieved his violin from one of the barrels and entertained the Captain and his crew with his music. The Captain was enchanted. When they docked at the lands to the east, rumors seemed to spread like the wind about the wonderful musician fished out of the sea. Everyone marveled at Timo, calling him a brave man for swimming behind the ship for two days and one night.

Everyone was in awe of Timo because of his adventure. "Tell us the story, Timo," was what Timo was asked regularly. Even Timo felt embarrassed, but he had to retell the invented story of his determination and bravery. Now all he wanted was to leave and get to the capital where no one would know about his fabulous swimming and stout heart.

In a few days of travel along the dirt road, he reached the capital. The capital was magnificent and splendid. The more he admired its riches, the more he fell into self-pity because of his poverty. Instead of feeling triumphant, he felt humiliated and lacked the confidence to play his violin for these wealthy-beyond-belief people.

He looked for some work in vain and grew depressed. Finally he was able to find a position as a cook's helper in the house of an extremely rich merchant. He could have never imagined such riches if he had not seen them with his very own eyes. The food was not just served on silver platters and eaten from golden plates, but it was cooked in silver kettles and fried in silver skillets and pans. Even dogs kept in the house were fed from silver bowls. Timo earned more in one month than he could have ever earned in one year at home.

Timo only grew more envious and greedier than ever. He felt all the treasures around him could never belong to him. He was tormented every time he saw a golden goblet and golden plate carried to the master's table.

For years Timo lived like this, hiding his jealousy. One Sunday afternoon, Timo dressed up in his finest clothes and went to the great garden in the city. As he strolled among all the strangers there, Timo saw a familiar face with a gray beard. He couldn't remember where or when he had seen this man or even who he was. The stranger was sitting alone under a linden tree. Timo wasn't sure if he would be recognized, but he went up to the familiar-looking stranger. Timo coughed to attract the attention of the man, then went right up to the man and greeted him. The stranger greeted Timo in return and abruptly asked, "Where is your violin?"

This familiar-looking stranger was none other than the traveler who had years ago advised Timo to become a musician. Timo told him his story, and the old man was visibly upset. "You are a fool. You were a fool when I first met you and you will always be a fool! What made you ignore your talent and become a cook's helper, scrubbing pots and pans? You could have earned more in one day as a musician than you are now being paid in half of a year. I am ordering you to run home and get your violin. Come back here and play and you will see that I am telling you the truth."

Timo did as he was ordered. When he returned with his violin, he sat on the bench beside his old friend and very reluctantly began to play. At the very first sounds Timo made on the violin, it seemed possessed. It almost seemed to be a new and unknown instrument to him. Never before had its tones been so rich, clear, and beautiful. Quickly a huge crowd gathered around the linden tree. Timo's melodies became more enchanting and sweeter than ever. To Timo's surprise, his old friend got up, took off his hat, and began to go among the listeners to collect money for the musician. Silver and gold coins fell as thick as a cloudburst into the hat from all sides. After a few more merry tunes, Timo left.

People in the garden called after him, "Come back again next Sunday to play for us, you amazing musician!"

At the arched gate of the city, the gray-bearded man told Timo, "Well, wasn't what you have just done far better than being a cook's helper? Again, I have pointed you in the right direction. Be clever and seize your luck with both hands! You must play under the linden tree every Sunday afternoon and entertain the people with your music. Buy yourself a top hat and place in it people's tokens of appreciation. Never refuse to play. Be contented with what people give you for your music. Most of all, though, do not become greedy! And now, we will meet again."

Shortly after this, Timo left the house of the merchant forever. Each Sunday he played in the city garden, and his audience as well as his earnings increased steadily. Timo prospered. His violin seemed to glow and sparkle in the sun and the streaming candlelight.

From afar the ruler of these rich eastern lands heard about Timo and how talented he was with his violin. He came once to the city garden to see for himself. After hearing Timo play, the ruler invited Timo to his palace to play for his court. When Timo did, the ruler gave him a bag full of gold. All of the nobles and wealthy people of the land followed the example of their ruler. Some of them even tried to surpass the ruler in generosity.

Timo became richer than he had ever dreamed he could be. After some years, he decided to return home. Now that he was a wealthy man he could afford to hire a ship to take him home with all of his treasures. Chests of gold, silver, coins, and jewels were loaded onto the ship. The wind was favorable and swiftly drove the ship into the open sea.

Towards night, when the ship was so far out that only the sky and water could be seen, a strong breeze rose. It grew into a raging storm. The sea lashed the foamy billows up to the sky, and the Captain wasn't able to keep the ship on course. The storm had become the master of the ship!

The ship was driven here and there by the sea for one day and two nights. It hit a huge rock and sank. The tiny lifeboats weren't able to survive in the wild sea, and all of the crew perished. Timo was the only one to survive. He hung onto a floating piece of timber and was tossed ashore by the waves. More dead than alive, Timo lay motionless on the rocky shore. Soon he slept.

While asleep he dreamed his gray-bearded friend visited him and gave him a drink that refreshed him and seemed to bring new spirit to him. When he awoke Timo found he was lying on a mossy rock, all alone. He went along the shore but he found the place was uninhabited. No one was there, not even animals. There was only deep forest with plants and trees that he had never seen before.

In distress, he sat down to think. What should he do? Suddenly vivid pictures of his past life floated before his eyes, and for the first time he realized how wrong he had been to leave home without the permission of his parents. He was also sorry that he had been so lazy for such a long time. "I guess I deserve to die in this strange place for what I've done and what I haven't done. I've even lost all of my treasures. I guess it's fitting that things so easily acquired were easily lost. My only regret is that my violin is also gone. I would have liked to have it to comfort me in my distress and to help make me feel better."

He started exploring his surroundings again and found an apple tree with beautiful red apples among the leaves. He tasted them and marveled. Never in all his life had he tasted such sweet and juicy apples. "Well," he thought, "I won't starve with these wonderful apples." He filled his pockets with fruit and continued on his way. After wandering for a long time he came to an open plain that seemed like an island in the woods. A burbling brook ran through it and beckoned to him. Timo hurried to the brook to drink some of the crystal-clear water.

In the water he saw his reflection and jumped up in terror, trembling like an aspen leaf. He saw himself disfigured and ugly, with big bags of flesh hanging from his nose.

"What is to become of me?" he wailed. The more he wailed, the bigger the bags of flesh on his nose grew. This ugly flesh turned blue like a furious turkey.

Nearby, there was a bush covered with appetizing nuts. Timo had always liked nuts, so even now, as he wallowed in self-pity, he picked a large handful of them. He cracked them with a rock and ate them. While he was eating he again looked at his reflection in the water and was overcome with joy to see that his nose was shrinking and shrinking. In a short time his nose was once again in its usual shape and usual place just a little bit above his mouth.

He was now curious to find out what had made his nose bloom so he ate another apple and kaboosh! His nose bloomed again. But when he ate more nuts, his nose returned to normal. "There may be some way this will be useful to me in the future," he thought as he filled his pockets with nuts. He even made a basket out of the bark of a tree and filled it with apples. He was now so exhausted that he lay down and slept the night under a tree.

Again, Timo dreamed that his gray-bearded friend came to him, gave him another drink, and told him to go back to the seashore. He seemed to tell Timo that he would be rescued. Before he left, the old man said, "Since you only regretted the loss of your violin, I will give you a new one as a reminder of me."

Timo recalled his dream in the morning. He looked around and sure enough—there lay the richest violin he had ever seen. He seized it and played to his heart's delight, forgetting his fears. He played until the forest echoed gaily in reply.

Timo reached the seashore when the sun was high in the sky. There he saw a ship anchored near the shore, with its crew busy making repairs. When one of the seamen saw Timo on shore he sent a boat out to bring Timo on board. All the sailors were as surprised to see Timo as he was to see them. After the repairs were completed, the ship set sail for the rich lands of the east.

"I thought I would never see this place again," Timo thought to himself. When they arrived, Timo disguised himself. He selected the nicest of the apples he had with him and went to the ruler's palace to sell them. One of the servants bought Timo's whole supply and paid him what Timo asked and more.

Timo knew what would happen from eating the apples, so he got out of there in a hurry. He found a place to stay in a place just outside of the city. Again he disguised himself, this time with a long black beard and mustache and foreign clothes, and told people that he was a foreign magician who was able to heal all diseases and defects.

The next day gloom hung over the city. Word had spread that a great disaster had struck the palace. The rumors were that the ruler and all his family had fallen ill after eating apples a servant had bought from a stranger. Physicians were summoned but all of them were baffled. Never before had they seen such a condition. They referred to it as a nose disease but refused to give anyone any details. Some physicians prescribed an immediate operation, but the ruler and his wife were afraid of losing their noses so they refused.

Word finally reached the palace of the ruler that a famous foreign magician was offering his services. Nobody recognized Timo in his disguise. Further, Timo's foreign accent was something no one had ever heard before. Timo was brought to the ruler and his family and pronounced them all to be afflicted with the turkey disease. He told them he could heal them without operating. He chopped up some nuts and gave each of them a teaspoonful of them. He ordered them to lie quietly in a dark room. They were to stay well covered and warm until they were cured. In a few hours, amazingly they were all healed.

The ruler was so full of joy he would have rewarded Timo with anything in his kingdom. But this was a new Timo. Since the shipwreck and loss of his treasures and his escape, Timo had also lost his former greed. He only accepted a small sum of money so he could buy an estate at home.

For the second and last time, Timo took leave of the rich land to the east. When he reached his own homeland, he bought a fine estate. Then he gave a feast to which he invited his family and all of his relatives. At the dinner table he said, "I am Timo. I am your former lazy son and brother, who caused such grief to you all. I left home without your permission but fortune has been kind to me. In fact, it has been much kinder than I deserve because I have returned a rich man." He invited all of his family to come and live on his estate.

Timo's father lived with him in his house. Later, Timo married a good, gentle maiden, whose only dowry was her beauty and her kind heart.

Timo was surprised on his wedding night, when he found his room crowded with chests and boxes containing all the treasures he had lost. He found a note in one of the chests: "To a good son who does not forget his parents and relatives. For his goodness, even the sea returns the treasures of which it had robbed him."

Timo never learned who his friend had been. Who had protected, guided, and helped him? Whoever it was, Timo's heart was empty of avarice and greed. ✠

The Amazing Towel

Long ago, in ancient times, fish were so plentiful around the shores of the Baltic Sea that fishermen caught them in their primitive nets more easily and in greater numbers than they do in these days.

In those days there was no lighthouse, nor steamers on the sea whose noise and movement now frighten all the fish away. The constant storms of our days, which sink and wreck the frail boats and tear the nets, were quite unknown in those ancient times.

How peaceful and beautiful was life in those old days. Fine spring days and warm autumn nights kept the fishing plentiful. With deepest worship, the fishermen venerated the Sea-Mother in their prayers and brought to her their humble offerings. This so pleased the Sea-Mother that she chose their shore for her dwelling place. Here in the lap of the gentle waves she built her palace and lived in undisturbed peace, protecting the fishermen and providing them with fish aplenty.

It is even said that an old fisherman from a village on the seacoast once had the great good fortune to see with his own eyes the wonderful palace of the Sea-Mother.

Late in the summer, one Sunday evening, a strange calm reigned over the sea. It was smooth like a mirror; not even the slightest ripple disturbed its still surface. Even though it was Sunday, two old fishermen decided to go fishing that night because they were short of fish. The two men were known as good workers, being always the first out on the sea and the last to return to the shore, but on this day, because it was Sunday, they did not enjoy their work. They pushed their boat into the water not far from

the place where a small brook joined the sea. In former times, it was said, there stood a church at that spot, until one day it suddenly vanished and sank into the sea. The people of the neighborhood still believe that the ringing of the church-bells, rising from the sea, can be heard at times.

The two men rowed out, spread their nets, and prayed to the Sea-Mother for her blessing. They prepared to cast their anchor, but it could not reach the bottom so they fastened a long rope to it, and then it sank down quickly. It settled just in the spot where the bells of the vanished church lay, and it struck the bells with a loud clang. The men filled their pipes, lit them, and sat down to smoke.

Suddenly, an unusual light appeared glimmering over the sea, not like the light that the seamen know well, foretelling a storm, but one they had never seen before. As they watched it, a strange feeling came over the fishermen. Their hearts were filled with a spiritual feeling such as one gets on a calm Sunday morning when going to church.

After a while, they lay down in the boat to rest. One of them had slept very little the previous night, and soon he began to snore. The other lay in the back of the boat thinking and watching. He was an old one-eyed man called Michael. He had his beloved kantele, or harp, with him, so while his companion slept, Michael played on his kantele. Some of the music he played was merry, and some was the sad melodies of the fishermen. He played them so beautifully that even the sea seemed to be listening sadly or joyfully according to his tunes. When his music stopped, the sea grew still, so still that the boat did not rock or move at all.

Suddenly the cool black sea rippled slightly, and Michael saw, not far from his boat, a pretty head rising from the water. After the head, there was a neck, and then a body appeared, until the whole image of a woman became visible.

Dusk descended rapidly, and it was almost dark. In spite of that, the image of the woman shone strangely. Michael could see clearly the unusual beauty of her face. Her long, curly, fair hair was adorned with the finest amber and pearls and other jewels. Michael clearly saw her green flowing robes of seaweed and her white apron, which was embroidered with red. Her apron was whiter than the most costly sails ever seen on the world's waters.

This amazing sight startled the kantele player, and he prepared to wake his slumbering companion, when the beliefs of the seamen came to his mind—that on the sea you never must show your companions what you see yourself and what the sea shows you, or great misfortune would befall you. So Michael kept still.

The wonderful woman approached the boat, smiled to Michael, and, in a voice that was as sweet as a flute, told him not to fear her because she was the Sea-Mother herself. She was the same Sea-Mother who rocked the fishermen when they were children on the waves and sent good luck to those who prayed to her and worshipped her with offerings. This day she was celebrating the wedding of her daughter with the Son of the Sun in the water-realm. When they returned home after the wedding ceremony they could not enter the palace, for the anchor of the two fishermen had fallen upon the threshold and blocked the entrance.

"Be kind and follow me to my water-palace, lift up your anchor, and then stay and play your kantele at my daughter's wedding celebration," begged the Sea-Mother.

Michael did not hesitate for a single minute, for he trusted the Sea-Mother completely, but the one thing that troubled him was how to get there. The Sea-Mother smiled, took him by his hand, covered his face with her apron, and helped him out of the boat. The waters opened before them, and they descended easily to the bottom of the sea.

The Sea-Mother lifted the apron from his face. Michael was blinded at first and dazed by what he saw. One of the Sea-Maidens brought some water and a towel and washed his face and rubbed his temples until he recovered and opened his eyes and was able to look around again.

What a miracle he beheld! What wonders greeted his eyes!

Before him lay the fantastic palace! It was made of glass, diamonds, pearls, beads, and shells and other marvelous materials not ever seen on earth. The walls were transparent like glass. The golden towers and gates glittered brilliantly. The crystal windows sparkled in their frames of precious pearls. In front of the palace the wedding procession stood waiting. All the inhabitants of the water realm seemed to be represented.

There were fishes and animals, mermen and mermaids, and even ugly sea monsters!

Before the gates stood a glittering chariot made of the prettiest seashells. The wheels flashed with fish scales. In the coach sat the bride and the bridegroom with sparkling crowns on their heads. The coach was drawn by giant fishes. They were the loveliest fishes of the sea. Helping them pull the coach were sea-pigs and sea-bulls.

The guests, different in color and shape, were riding on the backs of the biggest fishes, and they surrounded the coach. And just as the Sea-Mother had said, there at the entrance to the palace lay an old rusty anchor. Michael recognized it at once and hurried to remove it. The Sea-Mother opened the palace door with a diamond key and the procession entered the palace. Michael was invited to join the others.

Later, when Michael spoke of his adventure, he could not find enough words to describe the dazzling splendor of this marvelous palace. On the wedding table, among the rare and dainty dishes and the exquisite beverages, not even the simple, home-brewed beer of the coast-people was missing. It was served in transparent tankards made of amber.

The bride and bridegroom asked Michael to play the kantele for them. They hoped he would play it as beautifully as he had played it in his boat. Michael was amazed because he thought that no one was listening or watching as he played.

Michael played happily because for a musician to play his kantele at the wedding of the Sea-Mother's daughter was unheard of. All of the sea-people seemed to find great pleasure with his playing. The Sea-Mother herself was very kind to him and spoke to him encouragingly. She told him of her three royal sons who ruled the waters, one near the Islands, another near Finland, and the third somewhere far, far away. But here, of course, she herself ruled the sea.

The sparkling crown was lifted from the bride's head at midnight, and from an ornate chest she began to distribute gifts of remembrance to the guests. Her gifts were quite generous—beautiful shirts, stockings, gloves, and other fine handiwork that she herself had made in the long winter nights.

She didn't forget even Michael. Because he had come and played his enchanting music at her celebration, she gave him a beautiful, skillfully worked towel the like of which no mortal woman could ever make. It was whiter than the midwinter snow, embroidered with red, and had red fringes. The Sea-Mother's daughter herself wound it around Michael's kantele. Michael bowed low before her as he accepted her gift.

Following this, the Sea-Mother led him out, and, as before, she covered his eyes with her apron and took him back to his boat. In her silvery voice, with tones of great sadness, she asked him to tell the people of the coast that she had to depart from their waters and choose her dwelling elsewhere. She told him that many armed foreign warriors, speaking strange tongues, had come to these shores. These strangers plundered with fire and sword the people of her coast. The warriors brought noisy, troublesome boats that disturbed and muddled the waters. The constant vibration and roaring of these boats gave her no rest, not even in her own palace.

Great storms, bad times, poor fishing, and other misfortunes would come when she departed, but some day, she promised, she would come back to calm the storms and bless their lives and bring back the lost happiness to the people.

As she left Michael she bade him farewell and, nodding sweetly, slowly, very slowly sank back into the waves and was covered by the water.

For a while Michael looked after her, staring. Could all of this have really happened? Was it a dream or a vision?

No. It was real because the towel wrapped around his kantele assured him it was real. Michael turned to his companion, but he was still sleeping in the boat. Everything had happened so quickly far down in the water realm. Michael lingered until the rising dawn began to glow purple in the east. He awakened his companion and together they began to pull their nets out of the water. What a catch it was! Their nets were filled to overflowing with fish.

Michael's companion stood quite overcome with amazement. It seemed that this wonderful load would be too heavy for their old, frail boat. At last, with great difficulty, they reached shore.

After their work was done, Michael told the story of his wonderful experience on the sea to his companion. Michael's friend marveled at what he heard. He could not understand how Michael could possibly have attended the Sea-Wedding and have actually seen and conversed with the Sea-Mother in her palace in such a short time. But then he saw the wonderful towel around Michael's kantele, and he knew that Michael was telling the truth.

Hardly had Michael finished telling his story when, all of a sudden, the sad, quiet sea grew rough. The wind began to sigh strangely, and a storm rushed over the land, lashing the sea to fury and casting the foamy waves on the shore, like huge rocks. Yes indeed, the Sea-Mother had surely departed from these waters.

Michael removed his cap and stood with deep reverence. He bowed towards the sea and waved his hat in a sorrowful farewell. From that day on, devastating storms, rough seas, and poor fishing became the lot of the fishermen. It has continued like that to the present time. Only old Michael, the kantele player, had exceptional luck with his fishing to the end of his days. He liked to tell his story over and over again to his grandchildren in the long winter evenings while his feeble hands moved slowly, mending the nets.

The towel, the gift of the Sea-Mother's daughter, proved the truth of his story to all who would not believe. This towel was like no other on earth. It neither wore out nor could be soiled, though it was used constantly. Many cripples and sick were healed by it, and it became a custom at all weddings in the neighborhood to bind this towel around the gift-chest of the bride when the chest arrived at the bridegroom's house. Then everyone prayed and asked for the blessing of the Sea-Mother.

This amazing towel, the last gift of the Sea-Mother to her beloved people, was lost long, long afterwards. There was no trace of the towel, and it was never seen again. 🗙

A Jealous Love Enchantment

In a village above the Arctic Circle, in the land of the midnight sun, where the Lapps (or Sami) fish, tend their reindeer herds, and enjoy the amber-gold fruits of the cloudberry bushes in the summer, winters are another thing.

In the winter, the sun has abandoned the sky and is replaced by a season where the landscape appears in shades of grey made even more mysterious by ocean mists and the flashing Northern Lights. Legends tell of demons riding down from the hills on a fiery-red ray of the aurora borealis and descending on unsuspecting victims. Just before they strike there is a hissing, screaming, laughing, and cackling. These sheets of waving lights have been described as restless spirits playing and jumping about to and fro.

It was during this long, dark, mysterious time that the young people of the village were gathered in laughter and song. They were dancing and getting to know each other in an old musty building where the market people sold and traded their goods in the summer. On the walls of the building were carved many symbols for chasing away hobgoblins and bringing the occupants good luck, for these were a very superstitious people.

The demands of the summer, where night in and night out the men were on the sea fishing for codfish and salmon, or else tending their herds, or smoking fish and meat for the upcoming winter, were over. The women were free from gathering the amber cloudberries in the marshes from the patches of tall, pretty, five-fingered cloudberry

bushes with large crimson-greenish leaves, and preserving these gifts of nature for the long dark time coming.

A flickering candle of fish oil burned in the dance hall, revealing couples leaning against the walls or hugging as they sat on benches, dancing couples, and other playful young folks chasing each other. In the building were sounds of music, laughter, giggling, happiness, and joy.

Among the merrymakers was a most handsome Lapp fellow, Jussa, who was dressed in his white reindeer coat. He chanted primitive Lapp tunes quite loudly wherever he went. All the girls were eager to gain his attention. It was the dream of many of them to be his girlfriend. Jussa was able to enchant any girl with his singing and chanting jingles in honor of them.

There was only one girl that he was purposefully rude to in his songs. That was Elle Kuuva, the daughter of the old sorcerer. He made fun of her name and sang rhymes of "Koo koo Elle, lazy koo koo Elle, ugly lazy koo koo Elle."

Elle longed to be the special girl that would win Jussa's love. Once she had invited him to her home for supper that she had cooked herself. She hoped to impress Jussa with her wealth and skills. But Jussa only insulted her meal and even threw the reindeer meat and bones out of the door to an old glassy-eyed dog. He made up chants of disgust as he did this. As he left, Elle shouted from the door, "The evil spirits and dwellers in the nether world will come and get you for this." He only laughed, and she shook her fist at him and cried.

Elle Kuuva was among the crowd of young folks at the dance that night. While walking to the dance hall she had heard the scream of a lost soul in the hissing curtains of waving lights. She had learned enough sorcery from her father that she planned to use some this night to teach Jussa a lesson. If she couldn't have him, no one else could either.

She was one of the dark figures near the wall that night. She had a scornful smile on her face and hate showed in her eyes. Jussa never noticed her. He was busy charming the young girls.

The evening passed quickly, as it seems to do when people are enjoying themselves. It was close to midnight when a long, loud scream of anguish was heard from somewhere outside. Everyone in the hall stopped to listen. Fear was on every face but Elle's. Her sneer had turned to a look of joy and excitement.

Everyone knew the scream of a lost soul forebodes trouble and misfortune. Living with the sea, folks knew the sea spirits predicted bad things along with the weather. They had all heard these terrible sounds before. Some people believed they were not only sea spirits that they heard, but also the dead in their graves and the spirits of seamen who had been lost at sea.

The girls became frightened and ran to the door to go home, but the boys strutted bravely and would not let them go. Some were heard to say, "Don't worry. You'll be safe here with me. Come, let me put my arms around you for protection."

Slowly, the dancing and laughter returned and the Lapp chanting continued. Except, during all of this, Elle kept sneaking nervous glances toward the door.

The night was calm, but suddenly the whistling of the wind was heard on the other side of the door. The door bumped as the wind came up stronger, until suddenly the door bounced open with dust blowing up from the floor. The girls shrieked as a strange creature whirled in from the outside. It was a beautiful young girl in a rustling black silk dress. In the flickering oil light, her face was pale, but her eyes had a strange glow to them. The village girls backed away very timidly, and even the boys seemed less confident. Only Elle seemed to know the stranger, and she began to introduce the girl to the group. The girls moved aside while the fellows all crowded around the new girl.

Immediately, though, the girl seemed to float directly to Jussa. Jussa started to sing songs to the girl of her strange beauty. "Your eyes burn with fire and your black hair floats down your black silk dress. You are a special one." The room suddenly became oppressive, and the joy of the young people, all except Elle and Jussa, had turned somber. A gust of chilling wind blew into the hall and extinguished the flickering fish-oil lamp. There was a sound of swishing as the current of wind went up through the smokestack. Silence!

Except for the outburst of laughter from Elle Kuuva. The other girls were frantic and the boys nervous. The boys tried to relight the lamp, but their matches flared and died, and there were no comforting burning flames.

The girls stampeded to the door and rushed off into the night. Many were heard in loud prayer as they fled. The young men stayed and competed for the attention of the strange girl. They had no trouble finding her for though there was no light inside the room, her eyes glittered and glowed. They could also hear her heavy silk dress rustling. But she ignored all of the boys except for Jussa. Jussa chanted rhymes about her eyes.

All the while, Elle's laughter grated on everyone's ears. It was not happy laughter but much more nasty and mean.

Then the musty smell of a dead body floated in the hall. It became stronger and the boys now became frightened. They whispered that the girl must be some kind of earth spirit who had escaped from the cemetery. They fled, leaving the girl and Jussa alone in the room. The silk dress seemed to gleam like a shimmering ghost and rustled like a drifting breeze.

Jussa was hypnotized. He jabbered and jibbered and sang. Not a word of it made sense. The girl just beckoned to Jussa, and he awkwardly jerked the girl into his lap and hugged her. In return, she squeezed Jussa so tightly to herself that he seemed on the verge of suffocating. She bit him on his cheeks, ears, forehead, chin, neck, hands, and arms. At this Jussa became horrified and tried to scream but not a sound came out of his body. He shuddered when he felt the girl's skin. It was cold as ice, and her face was emaciated. He struggled and finally was able to shove the girl away.

But when they were separated, Jussa saw her glowing eyes enticing him in the darkness. He approached them and once more pulled her to his lap only to be seized by her. She seemed to emit a hissing sound as she clamped his body with the bony arms of a skeleton.

Again in terror, Jussa tried to break loose. There was a terrible struggle. They whirled, rolled, and lunged about in the room the whole time she bit, choked, and hugged Jussa. Objects in the room were knocked over with a clatter. Jussa smelled the odor of rotten death. Her eyes held him in her awful clutch.

Just as the first light of dawn weakly peeped from behind the bay, the girl released Jussa and drifted outside. The spell of her eyes led Jussa to follow her to the church. The Northern Lights were fading away.

Behind the church, they went through the gate to the cemetery. The girl was standing beside a weather-worn, tilted headstone. She still drew Jussa to her with her glowing eyes. She gave forth a long cry of sorrow, and just as Jussa was about to reach her, her clothes fell off her. Standing there, instead of a girl, was only a skeleton with empty eye sockets that gleamed. The skeleton began to shake and crumbled with a sharp clatter into a heap of bones.

Jussa could not understand all that had happened. He had visions of the silk dress, fiery eyes, and the sound of bones rattling against each other. As he stared at the spot in the cemetery, now all he could see was pure white unmarked snow.

He dug a hole all the way to the frozen ground with blood dripping from his torn fingers. He scraped the ice from the grave marker, moaning and sighing.

From that day forth, Jussa was looked upon as peculiar by everyone in the village. He had changed. There was no joy or teasing in him anymore. He stopped chanting his Lapp songs and poems. Instead, he wailed and cried.

The grave where he had last seen the skeleton was that of a young girl who had died a long, long time before. Stories told that it was the grave of a pretty young girl who had been buried in a black silk dress.

Meantime, while others feared Jussa, Elle Kuuva, daughter of the old sorcerer, always burst into mocking laughter when she saw him ranting and raving and moaning. ✠

The Holmolaiset Build a House

In a very remote part of Finland, there was a little village called Holmola. The people of Holmola, or the Holmolaiset, never traveled away from their town. They were happy there and had no need for anything else. Very seldom did anyone visit Holmola, so the people there became very set in their ways. You might even say they became quite different from the rest of the people in Finland. In fact, you might call them not only unique but weird. They became simple-minded and conservative.

Making decisions was extremely difficult for them as they pondered this way versus that way. They would talk, argue, discuss, and consider things for weeks before they ever got around to any action.

The Holmolaiset were rather like stories told about the Men of Gotham or the Fools of Helm. They were unpredictable and managed to make easy jobs difficult. These noodleheads would follow an idea to its extremes.

At this particular time, the Holmolaiset were getting ready for a new project. Everyone was arguing with each other and raising a ruckus. It had been like this for a year. It was all because the people got tired of living in houses shaped like wigwams. After a lot of discussion they decided to build houses that were different. They wanted to make houses using logs.

They organized people into teams for the different jobs. One team of Holmolaiset would cut down the trees, another group would trim the branches off and another bunch would peel the bark off of the trees. Another man would take out his homemade tape measure and measure the trees for the right length. There were men whose job

was to cut the tree into the measured lengths, and yet another gang would carry the logs to the place where the house was to be built.

Two fellows notched the ends of the logs so they would fit together tightly. It took four more men to lift the logs into place to make the walls. Women came along and chinked the places where the logs rested on each other with moss. When all the walls were up, the roofing group got to work.

Once they had decided how they would get the work done, they all worked on it. Slowly they worked, but carefully, until the log house was done. Then the workers went inside the finished house and closed the door.

"What has gone wrong?" they asked. They hadn't ever counted on it being pitch-black dark inside. After all, wasn't this log house built in the sunshine? "We chinked all of the walls so the sunshine would stay inside and not leak out," said the women.

The people all gathered together to solve this problem. What had happened to the sunshine? Where had it gone? They started to blame each other for making a mistake that helped the sun escape.

They brought in their local wise man to fix things and get the sunlight back. The wizard drummed on his drum while he chanted and sung spells to bring back the sun. He was a good wizard—the best they had. But his songs and chants, spells, and drumming didn't changed anything. It was still dark, dark, dark inside the house.

After several months of arguing, discussing, considering, and deciding, they felt that they had to carry sunlight into the house. This would be a very simple thing to do. All they had to do was to make great woolen sacks, fill them up with sunlight, twist the top of the sacks, and carry the sacks inside the house. Then they would open the sacks and let the sunlight fill the house.

Everyone worked hard to fill the house with sacks filled with sunlight, but when they opened the bags, nothing happened. It was still dark, dark, dark inside the house.

Just at this time a stranger named Matti happened to come to their town. Everyone was arguing and shouting. Matti asked them, "Is there something that I could help you with?"

The Holmolaiset told him what had happened and moaned about how everything had gone wrong, even after all of their careful planning.

"That's no problem, people of Holmola," declared Matti. "Where I come from we have been living in log houses with sunlight for a long time. I'll help you get the sunlight into the house if you pay me a 1,000 marks."

After a lot of loud bickering the people of the village agreed.

"Fine," said Matti. "Watch what I do," he told them. He walked into the house, kept the door open so he could see, took his axe from his belt and chopped out a square hole in the wall. When he was done, the sun streamed into the house and gave enough light that everyone could see all the empty sacks they had used, lying on the earthen floor. Everyone was delighted. They paid Matti and thanked him for his idea and his help.

Matti continued on his trip and no sooner was he out of the village limits and heading into the forest than the people got to arguing again. Since Matti's idea had worked so well they decided to improve upon it. Before they had properly discussed, argued, considered, and thought of all the possibilities, they set about improving the house. They started to hack out more windows in the house. They cheered as they saw more sunshine stream in the house. These noodleheads cut so many windows that before you could say "crash" the whole roof came tumbling down on their heads.

And that is why you will never find a log cabin in Holmola even to this day. The Holmolaiset keep telling the story of the time they let more sunshine in the log house and everyone learned from the story. No log houses in Holmola! ✠

Spirits of Karelia

There once was a brother, Pekka, and his younger sister, Vappu, who lived on an island near the Arctic Circle, in the Karelian part of Finland. Pekka and Vappu had six other brothers and sisters, but they were the two strawberry blondes in the family. All the other children had dry-straw-blonde colored hair. Their parents teased Pekka and Vappu that they had spent too much time eating cloudberries and strawberries—that must be why their hair had its reddish color.

They lived on a farm near the shore where the family raised hay, vegetables, potatoes, and flax along with farm animals. Other families lived on their island. Some of them were relatives while others were unrelated.

Their homemade boats were a regular part of life. People of the island even traveled to church on Sunday together in their longboats. Their area had hundreds of lakes, and Pekka and Vappu went out in their little boat to explore and fish often.

One day Pekka called, "Vappu! Put on your shoes and come help me spread some nets to catch salmon." Vappu quickly put some dry grass in her woven birch-bark shoes, snatched four fresh rice *piirakkaas* to eat (Karelians often carried piirakkaas for lunches), wrapped them in her scarf, stuffed them in her coat pocket, and ran after Pekka.

Pekka liked his feisty, eager little sister. They worked well together, but like all brothers and sisters, they teased each other regularly. Pekka took every chance he could to scare Vappu with stories of the spirits around them.

They pushed off in their boat and spread their nets in a place their father had taught them that the *lohi* (salmon) liked. They left the nets there and visited some other islands to look for berries. There was a group of islands further out that Pekka never landed on; in fact, he was careful to avoid them.

"Why don't we ever look for berries on those islands over there?" asked Vappu.

"Those are the Devil's Islands. I don't think we want to go there," answered Pekka.

"What's the matter? Are you scared to go just because the islands are called Devil's Islands?" teased Vappu.

"Of course not!" snapped Pekka. "Their name has nothing to do with it. You don't see grownups going there either, do you?" Pekka didn't want his sister to think he was a coward. After all, didn't his parents trust him with the double sheath knife when he was quite young? His father made him memorize the directions for its use before he gave it to Pekka. They were:

> *The small one spreads your butter,*
> *nicely cuts your leg of mutton,*
> *cleans your pipe,*
> *disciplines the kids.*
>
> *The big one is for feast intended:*
> *baptism, wedding,*
> *burial, churchgoing.*
> *It further comes to use*
> *whenever momentous differences of opinion*
> *need to be settled*
> *between grownup men.*

Being the owner of the double sheath knife must mean Pekka was brave enough to follow the directions for the use of the two different sharp knives.

Vappu persisted: "Why doesn't anyone go there? They look like lovely islands."

Pekka said, "Let me tell you an old story and then see if you want to visit the islands, especially the bigger one with the mountain on it. There is an old story that goes like this. There was a lake in which there was an island, in which there was a lake, in which there was an island, in which there was a lake, in which there was an island.... The devil lives on one of the islands. There was a cave in the mountain and it had a lake in it. The devil lives there. He had such long legs that he was able to jump from island to island to island. He used the islands to travel across big lakes. When he isn't traveling or sleeping he loves to make big storms. He whips up huge waves that crash over the shore and swamps boats and drowns people. Whenever storms hit people in Karelia, we know the devil is on a rampage, and everyone warns each other to be careful and avoid Devil's Islands. That's how the islands got their name. Now do you want to go visit there?" demanded Pekka.

"Has anyone ever seen the devil?" pesky Vappu asked.

Pekka just grunted in exasperation at her question.

"Well, all the grownups are also telling us about the hiisi. Just this morning Mother told me to be careful because the hiisi was out there and might try to capture us. She told me she would miss us terribly if the hiisi got us and that we should be careful," mused Vappu.

"I have never seen a hiisi," answered Pekka, "but I have heard them hiss, and they don't sound like something I want to meet."

Pekka and Vappu rowed back to their nets and dragged them in carefully. They hauled in a good day's catch of salmon. "Looking at all these fish reminds me that I'm hungry," moaned Pekka.

"I knew that would happen," said Vappu. "You surprised me, though, that you waited this long to be hungry. Maybe it was the hiisi talk that made you forget food." As she was saying this she slowly unwrapped the four rice piirakkaa she had wrapped in her scarf. They each nibbled slowly on these wonderful little pies.

Pekka and Vappu cleaned the fish and got them ready for their father to smoke. There was nothing better than smoked salmon. Some of the salmon had eggs in them, and they were careful to collect them so they could be salted and turned into caviar. Vappu especially liked the caviar on hard bread. The tiny eggs popped when she bit down into them.

Because they lived in the land of the midnight sun, there was still light out after supper. They walked over to the stream with the water lilies on it. "I know why the water lily is called the nakki-rose," said Vappu as they picked some of them. "The nakki uses the stem and flower of the water lily as a lure."

"You're right, Vappu. The nakki sits at the bottom of lakes and streams and fishes for people. No one knows what a nakki looks like, but it will pull children under water and drown them."

"Have you ever seen one, Pekka? Let's look and see if we can find one."

"No, I haven't," Pekka said. "But I've heard the water ripple and seen the waves from a water lily that looked as if the nakki was wanting me to catch it."

Many years passed. Wars tore at their lands and family. Karelia was taken as a prize, and the beautiful island farm was burned to the ground. Family members tried to cross from their beloved Karelia into free Finland. Some never made it across the new border; they disappeared and were never heard from again. But Pekka escaped with an uncle to Finland, and Vappu also made it into Finland with another family from their island.

Many years later, Pekka and Vappu were reunited. They were now both old, and their hair was no longer strawberry blonde, but some things never change. Vappu still looked to Pekka for love and wisdom. On one especially bright midnight sun evening, she finally confessed to Pekka that "I never believed in the devil, the hiisi, or the nakki. Not really. But I do think I heard them somehow a long time ago."

*T*raditional *K*arelian Rice *P*iirakkaa

Crust

    1 cup water   1½ cups white flour

    1 teaspoon salt   1½ cups rye flour

    2 tablespoons melted butter

Filling

    1 cup uncooked medium-grain rice   2 tablespoons butter

    2 cups milk   (Additional milk if necessary to thin out filling)

Glaze

    ½ cup butter, melted

    ½ cup hot milk

Topping

    1 cup softened butter

    4 hard-boiled eggs, chopped

For the crust, mix the water, salt, and melted butter in a large bowl and stir in the white flour. Beat until smooth. Add the rye flour and mix until well blended. Turn the dough out onto a floured board and knead until smooth (about 2 or 3 minutes). Shape the dough into a roll about 2 inches in diameter, divide into 12 equal portions, and dust with flour. Pat each into a small round cake, then roll out into a circle about 6 to 8 inches in diameter, keeping the shape as round as possible.

For the filling, combine the rice, salt, and milk in the top of a double boiler. Cook over boiling water, stirring occasionally, for 2 hours or until the milk is absorbed and the rice is creamy. Stir in the butter.

For the topping, mash butter and hard-boiled eggs together until blended.

Heat the oven to 450 degrees F. Spread rice filling in a three-inch strip across the center of each dough circle almost to the edge. Fold opposite sides over filling. Leave an inch of filling exposed in the center. Crimp each edge by pinching to form an oval and seal in the filling. Place the piirakkaa on greased baking sheets.

For the glaze, mix the butter and hot milk and brush the mixture lightly over the piirakkaa during the baking. Bake 15 minutes or until light brown. Remove from the oven and brush again with the glaze mixture.

Serve hot or cold with egg butter spread over the top.

This recipe makes 16 piirakkaa.

Kurt, Brooke, Andrea, and Emily Livo sharing piirakkaa.

The Enchanted Wood of Karelia

In the olden days, there was in the land of Karelia a pretty forest that was warmed by the gulf stream currents. No human being dared to enter it because, as people said, those who had chanced to come to the borders of the wood had seen a tumbledown house under thick trees. Swarming around this house was a host of ragged, sooty, human-like beings, like ants in an ant hill.

One dark night, a peasant coming home from a feast lost his way and wandered into this forest. There he beheld an amazing thing indeed! Around a blazing bonfire there was a crowd of women and children. Some of them sat on the ground while the others danced about.

An old woman, who had an iron ladle in her hand, scattered hot ashes over the grass from time to time. When she did this, the children would rise high up into the air, fluttering around like owls, and then settle down again.

Out of the wood came a little old man with a long gray beard and a big sack on his back. The sack was bigger than the man was. The women and children immediately ran to meet him with loud shouts. They whirled around him and tried to pull his sack down, but somehow he managed to shake them off.

The next thing the peasant saw astounded him. A big black cat, as large as a foal, sprang from the threshold upon the old man's sack, and together they disappeared inside the house.

In all honesty, the peasant was not in such good shape himself because his head was dull from excessive feasting, so everything appeared double to his eyes.

Maybe that was the reason no one could be sure what part of his story was true and what was not.

From generation to generation however, similar stories circulated about this Karelian forest, but nothing definite was ever learned. Around this time the King of Sweden gave orders to destroy the mysterious wood, but the people dreaded to fulfill his command. It was said that a bold man had struck one of the trees with his axe, and blood began to ooze from the tree and a cry was heard as if someone were in great pain. The man fled terrified and trembling all over. After that, nothing could tempt the woodcutter to enter that Karelian forest or to touch a tree in it.

Not far from the forest was a big village. Here, a peasant widower had recently married again, and, as so often happens, he brought into the house an ill-tempered, quarrelsome woman. He had a little seven-year-old daughter, Liisa, from his first marriage. Liisa was bright and had a very lively imagination.

Liisa's cruel stepmother made life unbearable for her. She scolded and beat the girl daily, from morning to night. The food she gave to Liisa was worse than the scraps from the table that she fed to her dogs. The father was a worn-out weakling and could not defend his child. In fact, he himself danced to the shrill piping of his wife. For more than two years Liisa suffered misery and want, and in her trouble she secretly shed many bitter tears.

One Sunday Liisa went berry picking with the other village children. As they roamed around from bush to bush, the children came to the borders of the mysterious forest. They didn't know where they were because they didn't pay attention to anything but the berries. The strawberries they found growing there were the finest they had ever seen! The grass was red with them! The children sprawled out on the grass and ate the delicious berries. They filled their bark baskets with all the strawberries they could hold.

Suddenly, one of the eldest children recognized the dreaded place and he shouted, "Run! Run! We are in the enchanted forest!" At these words, the children ran as if all the ghosts of the forest were after them.

Liisa had gone deeper into the wood than the other children and had just found the sweetest berries under the bushes. She heard the shouts of the boy, but she did not want to leave the berries. "The people in this forest can be no worse than my stepmother!" she thought.

Just then a little black dog with a silver bell around its neck came running up to her, barking loudly. Following the dog was a little girl, dressed in rich silk. "Be quiet," she ordered the dog. To Liisa she said, "I am glad you did not run away with the other children. Stay here and keep me company! We can play nicely together and gather berries every day. I hope my mother agrees and does not object when I ask her permission. Come, let us go at once to my mother."

The strange child took Liisa by her hand and led her deeper into the forest. The little black dog barked now for joy. It jumped at Liisa and licked her hands just as if they were old friends.

What wonders and splendor greeted the eyes of little Liisa. She was sure that she was in heaven! She saw a beautiful garden with fruit trees and bushes in front of her. On the branches of the trees sat wonderful birds. These birds were richer in color than the brightest butterflies. Some of them were covered with gold and silver feathers that shone in the light. The birds were so tame that the children could take them in their hands. In the middle of the garden stood a grand house made of crystal and precious stones. It glittered like the sun!

A lady in fine clothes sat on a bench at the entrance to the house. She said, "Who is the child you are bringing home with you, my daughter?"

The strange child replied, "I found her alone in the woods and I brought her home. She can keep me company. May she stay with us? It is so lonely sometimes for me."

The mother smiled but didn't speak. She examined Liisa from head to heels. Then she invited Liisa to come nearer. She stroked Liisa's cheeks and asked her about her home. "Are your parents alive? Would you like to stay here?"

Liisa kissed the woman's hand, fell on her knees and said, bursting into tears, "For a long time my mother has rested under the grassy earth. My father still lives but what good does it do when my stepmother hates me? Nothing I do pleases her. Dear gracious lady, let me stay with you! Let me tend your cattle or give me some other work. Gladly I will do everything and obey you always. Only, please do not send me back to my stepmother! She will beat me to death because I stayed away longer than the other children."

The lady smiled and said, "We shall see what I can do for you then." She rose and went into the crystal house.

"Have no fear, my mother is kind!" said the little girl. "I saw by her looks that she will grant our wish. She first has to think it over." The little girl told Liisa to wait, and followed her mother into the house. Liisa trembled with hope and fear at the same time. The minutes of waiting seemed endless in her anxiety to learn what the lady would decide.

After what seemed like ages, the little girl returned with a small box in her hand. "My mother said we should go and play today until she makes up her mind about you. I hope you will be able to stay with us, for I should be very sorry if you go. Have you ever been on the sea?"

Liisa's mouth and eyes opened wide with surprise. "On the sea? What is that? I have never heard of such a thing."

"Soon you will see it," replied the girl. She opened the small box, which contained a leaf, a shell, and two fish bones. A few dewdrops were glittering on the leaf, and the little girl spilled them on the ground. Instantly the garden, the pretty lawn, and everything around them vanished. As far as eyes could see there was nothing but sky and water. Only under the children's feet a patch of firm land remained.

The little girl set the shell on the water and took the fish bones in her hands. The shell swelled and grew into a fine big boat that could easily hold a dozen children. The two girls stepped into the boat. Liisa stepped in timidly, but the other girl got in with a rollicking happy-go-lucky air. The fishbones in her hands changed into oars. The waves tossed them along as if they were in a cradle and carried them on and on. Little by little, other boats came sailing up filled with people who laughed and sang merrily.

"We must sing to them in turn," said the little girl. Liisa did not know how to sing, but the other child sang beautifully. Liisa could not understand what they were singing, but she noticed that they often repeated the word "Annika." She asked her companion what it meant and was told, "That is my name."

They did not know how long their pleasure ride had lasted when they heard a voice calling, "Children come home! It will soon be dark!"

Annika took the box from her pocket and dipped the leaf into the water so that a few drops of water remained on it. Instantly they were back in the beautiful garden, near the splendid house. No traces of water were to be seen. Annika put the leaf, the shell, and the fish bones back into the box, and the two little girls went into the house.

In a large room around a large table were twenty-four ladies. They were all dressed in gorgeous robes as if they were at a wedding feast. At the head of the table, on a golden chair, sat Annika's mother. Liisa wished she had more eyes to admire all of this beauty! The table was set with thirteen gold and silver dishes, but one of the dishes remained untouched. Not even its cover was lifted during the meal.

Liisa enjoyed the dainty food, which tasted better to her than the sweetest cakes she had ever eaten. At the table, conversation was carried on in low voices and in a strange language. Liisa did not understand a single word of what they were saying. At length, Annika's mother said something to the maid who was standing behind her golden chair. The maid hurried out. In a moment she returned with a little old man whose beard was longer than himself. The little old man bowed low and waited at the door. The lady pointed to Liisa and said, "See this village child, whom I intend to adopt. Make me an image of her to send to her village in her place."

The little old man looked at Liisa with an expert eye, as if taking her measure, bowed again, and left. When the meal was over, the lady said to Liisa, "Annika begged me to let you stay here to be her playmate. You yourself also said that you would like to stay with us. Is this true?"

In her gratitude, Liisa fell to her knees and kissed the lady's hands and thanked her with all of her heart. The lady lifted her up and stroked her hair. As she patted Liisa's cheeks she said, "If you will always be a good and obedient child you will be happy. The best care will be given to you here until you grow up and can shift for yourself. My young ladies, who teach Annika, will instruct you also. They will teach you all manner of fine handiwork and other useful things."

As the lady was saying this, the little old man returned. On his shoulder he carried a trough filled with clay. In his left hand he held a little basket covered with a lid. He set these objects on the floor and took a piece of clay into his hands. He began to model a doll that soon took the shape of a real child.

The body of the doll was left hollow. In it he put three small fishes and a piece of bread. In the doll's breast, the little old man made a hole. He took a black snake from his basket and let it wriggle into the hole. Then the lady examined the doll from all sides. The little old man said, "Now we do not need anything else except one drop of the village child's blood."

Liisa grew pale as she listened to this because she thought that if she gave a drop of her blood she would sell her soul to the evil one. But the lady comforted her, saying, "Have no fear! We do not want your blood for evil but only for your own good and for your future happiness."

As she said this, she took a fine gold needle, pricked Liisa's arm, and gave the needle to the little old man. He stuck the needle where the doll's heart should be. Then he placed the doll in the basket and promised to come the next morning to show the results of his work.

After he left, everyone went to bed. A chambermaid took Liisa to her bedroom, where a soft bed of goose feathers with silken covers and downy pillows was made up for her. Even the chamber pot under the bed was made of solid gold.

The next morning, when Liisa awoke, she found herself wearing a gown as fine as air. The loveliest clothes lay on a chair beside her bed. A maid came and told Liisa to wash her face and comb her hair. Soon Liisa was dressed from head to heels in beautiful clothes as if she were a child of noble birth. Nothing pleased Liisa more than the shoes! Until this moment she had gone barefooted or wore shoes made of birch bark. She was certain that not even the king's daughters could have nicer shoes than she!

Her old clothes had been taken away and Liisa soon learned why. They had been put on the figure of clay that was to take her place in her old village. During the night in a secret chamber, the doll had grown, and in the morning it looked just like Liisa. It even could run around like any other child. Liisa was very much frightened to see this perfect copy of herself, but Annika's mother reassured her. "Be not afraid! Clay cannot harm you. We will send this image to your stepmother for her to beat instead of you! She may beat it to her heart's content, for the image of clay will feel no pain. But if the wicked woman does not change for the better, then someday your image will punish her as she deserves."

From that time on, Liisa lived a happy life as if she were the petted child of noble parents and had been rocked in a golden cradle. Trouble, toil, and sorrow became a thing of the past for her. Even her studies grew easier day by day and her former misery seemed only a bad dream to her.

The more Liisa lived in her new surroundings, the queerer everything appeared to her. All the strange things that she saw here could not come to pass naturally. She was sure that a magic power must be ruling over life here.

A big granite stone stood about twenty steps from the entrance to the crystal house. Before every meal the little old man went to the stone, took a silver rod from his chest pocket, and tapped the stone with it three times until it rang in response. Instantly a golden cock sprang out from under the rock and seated himself on the top of it. Every time the cock crowed or flapped his wings, something appeared from under the stone.

First came a large table provided with just as many place settings as there were people. The table moved into the house by itself as if carried on the wings of the wind. At the cock's second crowing, out came chairs that followed the table into the house. One after another, dishes filled with food leaped out and settled on the table. Then came apples, berries, and bottles of mead. Everything seemed alive, and no servants were needed to carry the food and to wait at the table.

When the meal was over, the little old man tapped the stone again with his silver rod and the golden cock crowed for the table and all the bottles, dishes, plates, and chairs to return under the stone. But when the thirteenth dish came, the one that was never touched, a big black cat followed it, sat beside it on the stone next to the cock, and stayed there until the little old man came to carry them all away. He took the dish in his hand, the cat under his arm, and the cock on his shoulder, and vanished with them under the stone.

Not only food and drink but also clothes and all kinds of household goods leaped out from under the stone when the golden cock crowed.

One day Liisa asked Annika why the thirteenth dish appeared on the table every day although no one ate from it. Annika could not tell her, but she asked her mother about it. In a few days the lady sent for Liisa and said to her very earnestly, "Do not trouble your heart with vain thoughts that will bring you no good. You want to know why we never eat from the thirteenth dish? I can only tell you that we dare not touch it or our happiness would come to an end."

The years passed by with the speed of the wind. Liisa grew up to be a lovely maiden. Annika, on the other hand, was the same little child she was when they first met in the wood. The young ladies, the companions of Annika's mother, daily instructed Annika and Liisa in reading and writing and in all kinds of handiwork. Liisa's progress was good, but Annika often preferred childish play to useful work. When a playful mood took hold of her, Annika would throw aside her work, seize her little box, and run out to play "sea," and no one would mind. Sometimes she said to Liisa, "What a pity that you have grown so big and can no longer play with me."

And so nine years passed. One evening the lady sent for Liisa to come to her bedroom. Liisa was surprised because the lady had never called her before at such a late hour. Her heart beat like a captured bird in her breast and seemed ready to burst. When she entered the room, Liisa noticed that the lady's cheeks were red and her eyes were full of tears.

"Dear beloved child," began the lady, "the time has come for us to part."

"Part?" cried Liisa, falling on her knees before the lady. "No, no! Dear lady, surely that is not possible. Only death has the power to part us. I beseech you to have pity on me and do not drive me away. I want no other happiness than to live with you until I die."

"Say no more, dear child. My heart aches within me, but it is inevitable that everything must happen as I tell you. You are a mortal and some day your life will come to an end. Therefore you cannot remain here any longer. Though I and all the others who are around me appear in human shape, we are not humans but higher beings whom people cannot know. In a country far away you will find a loving husband who is waiting for you. It is not easy for me to part with you, but it must be. You must accept your fate."

The lady combed Liisa's hair with a golden comb and sent her to bed. How could poor Liisa fall asleep after what she had been told? Life seemed desperately dark and hopeless to her.

In the meantime the clay image had replaced Liisa in her father's house in the village. The image, which did not feel any pain, endured without a murmur all the cruelty of the wicked stepmother. She beat and abused the clay image both day and night.

Then one day the stepmother again tormented the clay image, and in her rage she seized the image by the throat to choke it. The black snake darted out hissing and stung the stepmother in her tongue. She instantly fell dead to the ground.

When the husband came home in the evening he found his wife lying on the floor, swollen like the stump of a tree. His daughter was nowhere to be seen. The man called and shouted until the neighbors came. They had heard screams coming from the house at noon, but as such things were of daily occurrence there, no one paid any more attention than usual. In the afternoon all had become quiet again, but no one had seen the child.

Tired from his day's work, the husband retired to his bedroom. He must have thanked his good fortune that at last he was rid of the woman. On the table he found three small fishes and a crust of bread. He ate them for his supper and went to bed. The next morning he too was found dead, his body as swollen as that of his wife. A few days later they were both buried in the same grave. Now they would not quarrel any more. Their daughter had vanished completely and was never seen again.

And what of Liisa? She had not closed her eyes the whole night and wept bitterly over the coming parting. In the morning the lady gave her a seal ring and hung a gold locket around her neck from a silken ribbon. The lady called the little old man and sadly took leave of her before Liisa had time to thank her.

The little old man tapped Liisa's head with his little silver rod three times. Liisa felt herself changing into a bird. Her arms turned into wings, and her legs became eagle legs with long strong claws. Her nose became a hooked beak and feathers covered her body. She rose and soared through the air below the clouds just like a real eagle.

For many days she flew towards the south, resting her tired wings now and then but feeling no hunger. Then one day, as she hovered low over a forest where hounds were barking, a sharp arrow suddenly pierced her wing. In fear and pain she dropped down in a swoon.

When she had recovered her senses and opened her eyes again, she found herself lying under a bush in her human form. How had she come here? All the other strange things that had happened to her seemed but an obscure dream.

Then she saw a handsome young prince riding towards her. He sprang from his horse, gave her his hand in greeting, and said, "At a lucky hour did I set out from home this morning! Of you, beloved maiden, I have dreamed every night for half a year. I knew that I would find you here in this forest. Hundreds of times I have tramped this road in vain, yet I did not lose hope. Today I shot an eagle who must have fallen nearby, and while searching for the bird I found—you!"

He lifted her up into his saddle and together they rode to the city where the old king welcomed them. A few days later they got married. On the morning of the wedding day, fifty cartloads of costly things arrived for Liisa from her kind foster mother.

After the death of the old king, Liisa became queen. When she grew old she liked to tell the story of the adventures of her childhood and youth. But no one has ever since seen or heard of that enchanted wood of Karelia.

 *How the Riihi Mies Got Rich*

Once a rich landowner had a skillful and successful *riihi mies* (or overseer) for his *riihi*. The riihi was a three-section barn that was used for the drying and thrashing of the grain. The riihi mies took care of everything there for the landowner.

There was one particular fall, though, when one mishap after another followed the riihi mies. Each time he came to settle accounts with the miller, there was a shortage, and the landowner was upset by it. In his anger he ordered the riihi mies to be whipped.

After one of these particularly hard days at the landowner's manor, the riihi mies was sitting on a bench beside the kiln, worrying about his problems. He knew he was innocent, and the more he sat and thought about what was happening, the more frustrated he became, until he began to swear and curse aloud.

From somewhere behind him he heard a voice asking, "What is the matter with you, friend?"

The uninvited voice belonged to the mischievous character Old Pagan, who had supernatural powers. Not only was Old Pagan tall, stout, and strong, but he was also a simpleton, and everyone knew he could be very easily outwitted.

"What is the matter, yes indeed, what is the matter?" he replied sullenly. "Every time I settle accounts with the miller, I am short of grain. I end up paying for the loss myself and even then I get a whipping ordered by my master."

"I will take pity on you, poor fellow," said Old Pagan. "Here is a sack. Take it and fill it with grain and put it in the corner of the granary. As many times as you tap it with the heel of your left foot, there will be so many sacks of grain left over at every measuring time, and this extra grain will be yours to sell." With this advice, Old Pagan left.

The riihi mies was excited by this possibility and immediately tried it out. Behold! After tapping the sack with his left heel three times, three sacks of grain were left over! The man was happy, and he sold the extra grain for an amazing amount of money. While all of this was happening, his master was again pleased with his work.

There was still one problem. The riihi mies could not get rid of Old Pagan now. Every night, there by the kiln sat Old Pagan, and he stayed until the cock crowed. While he sat there he played tricks on the riihi mies and teased him unmercifully. For instance, when the riihi mies baked potatoes or turnips, Old Pagan was always the first to eat them. When the man brought some meat or other tidbit from home, Old Pagan stole them from him.

Now the riihi mies had something new to complain about. Once when he was sitting at the inn, he complained to his companions about his problems with Old Pagan. It happened that a fellow, who was called Bear-Dancer because he earned money dancing with his trained bear, was sitting in the corner at the inn and heard the riihi mies's story. "I know a remedy," Bear-Dancer remarked. "Take my bear Karhu with you and hide him somewhere in a corner. Then, pick a quarrel with Old Pagan and call the bear to help you."

The riihi mies was pleased with this plan and took the bear to the threshing barn that very night. Before Old Pagan appeared, the riihi mies took advantage of the time to bake some turnips.

It was not much longer before Old Pagan made his appearance. Old Pagan picked out all of the turnips that were baked and ate them and taunted the riihi mies:

> *"What is baked is mine,*
> *What is raw is thine."*

and he threw away all of the unbaked turnips. The riihi mies tried to stop him but could not, so in frustration he picked up the raw turnips and threw them back at Old Pagan. Some of them struck Old Pagan's head.

"Stop that or I will give you a good thrashing!" threatened Old Pagan. When the man did not stop, Old Pagan jumped up in a fury and began beating the riihi mies on his back.

"Karhu, dear bear, help! Help!" screamed the man.

With a leap, Karhu was at his side. In a fury the bear clawed and scratched Old Pagan until he begged, "Do what you will. Quarrel as much as you want to, only do not scratch my face and my eyes."

The riihi mies found that it was no easy thing to calm the angry bear. While he was trying to quiet the bear, Old Pagan took the chance to escape. He had learned his lesson with the bear and never came back to trouble the riihi mies again.

"Ah!" sighed the relieved man. "This is too good to be true!" He gave the Bear-Dancer many sacks of grain as a reward for his advice and help.

Some time later, Old Pagan was wandering about the landowner's manor. As he passed the shepherds he asked, "Do you know, or have you seen, if the riihi mies of the manor has his black cat still?"

The shepherds knew quite well that the riihi mies had a black cat, but they had never heard anything about the bear attack, so they said, "Yes, his cat is still alive. In fact she just had three young ones."

"If that is so, I can never return. What a pity that I forgot my purse on the edge of the kiln, and now I cannot hope ever to get it back," complained Old Pagan to himself.

The shepherds heard him mumbling and told the riihi mies what Old Pagan had asked them and what he had said. The riihi mies hurried to the kiln and there he found a big bag heavy with gold. Oh happy day! Now the riihi mies was richer than even his own master. With Old Pagan gone, the riihi mies had nothing to do except enjoy the rest of his life with his new riches. ✠

The Wolf with the Burning Eyes

When the great magician created the Earth and everything on it, he asked the evil spirit, "What do you think of my work? Is it worthy of praise? Maybe you think some useful animal or some important plant is lacking? Maybe it seems to you that the mountains are not high enough and the waters not deep enough? Are the birds attractive? Is there anything missing that you can think of?"

The evil spirit was pleased to be asked for his opinion. Gathering all of his courage he said, "Your work is not to be blamed, but there ought to be one animal more who would be able to protect the forests against the thoughtless shepherds who so often break the branches, peel the trees, and kill young hares and goats."

The great magician was surprised by this answer. "I put the bear and creeping snake in the woods for this very purpose. Aren't they enough?"

"Have you considered that in the winter these guards fall asleep? It is always so sad to see the forests and the creatures in it left unprotected like poor orphans. If you agree, I would like to create this needed animal myself. There is only one favor that I would ask, though. Since I do not have the magic power to give life to the thing I create, would you give me such a magic word? My creation, I promise, will not be worse than yours!"

The great magician replied quickly, "Yes, that I will promise you. When your animal is finished, mouth and eyes put in their right places, then say, 'Get up, and devour the evil spirit.' "

"The devouring will not be for some time yet," thought the evil spirit, and he disappeared into the depths of the woods. There he gathered stones, twigs, and soft green moss. He brought from the village blacksmith, two fiery sparks, and many nails. In the darkness of the night he started his work.

He used a strong hedge pole for the backbone. For the head he chose a tree stump. He made the body out of bricks and twigs and used a large fern for the tail. Alder sticks were fashioned into feet. Where the heart should have been, he placed a stone. He covered the whole body with the moss and put the fiery sparks in for eyes. The iron nails became claws and teeth.

Observing his work, the evil spirit was pleased and gave his creature the name "Wolf." But the Wolf had not yet been given the breath of life. The evil spirit remembered the instructions of the great magician earlier and said, "Wolf, get up and devour—" but before he could finish the words the Wolf leaped up!

The evil spirit was frightened by this but soon recovered himself and got ready to continue with his evil doings. He said to the Wolf, "Wolf, get up and devour the great magician."

Nothing happened. The Wolf did not move even the tip of his tail. The evil spirit repeated his order to the Wolf many times, but the Wolf never twitched a muscle.

The evil spirit went back to the great magician and told him that he had created a creature he called Wolf. "I do not seem to have the right commands that give life to the Wolf and make him move."

The great magician looked at the evil spirit calmly and asked, "No?" Did you say, 'Get up and eat the evil spirit?' "

The evil one never expected such an answer and even he became ashamed of himself for the lie he had told the magician. Without another word, the evil one went back to his created creature and gave the right order. He gave it in a very low, soft voice. What happened next was so quick that the evil one was caught right in his tracks. The Wolf became alive and jumped up and chased the evil one. The Wolf ran like the wind and would have caught his creator and eaten him, but the evil one hid himself under a large stone.

From that time on, the Wolf became the fiercest enemy of the evil one. His backbone is immovable, just like a pole without joints. His teeth and claws are sharp like iron nails. His eyes glitter like fiery sparks, and his skin is covered with thick fur. The Wolf's heart is still made of stone, and the Wolf has no pity. He steals and eats poor innocent lambs.

When you are in the forest in the fall and you happen to see the Wolf's burning eyes, you must know that he is still searching for his enemy—the evil one!

Why the Wolf Became Malicious

In the old, old days the wolf was not the wicked wild beast we now think of him. He was as tame and friendly as family dogs. Once, though, a nasty farmer's wife threw a red-hot stone to the wolf instead of his usual food. The wolf ran away from people, and to this day he has been a crafty, mean beast.

The wolf's jaws were terribly burned by the hot stone. For a long time after that, he and his fellow wolves got their food from Heaven. One day at meal time, one of the wolves was overlooked and didn't receive any food. He complained bitterly of this injustice.

Heaven responded to his complaints, "Eat him whom you meet first!" The hungry wolf trotted off in search of his food. The first person he met was a ragged, skinny beggar.

"Heaven told me to eat you!" snarled the wolf to the beggar.

"Dear wolf," pleaded the beggar, "I would make a bony mouthful for you. All I am is bones and rags. Why don't you wait for a tastier, younger, juicy mouthful?"

"You are quite right!" thought the wolf to himself. "An old creature like this is worth nothing. I will look further for a really tasty morsel."

To the beggar's surprise the wolf said most graciously, "I grant you your wish! Go!"

The wolf trotted along the trail and soon he met a woman. "You look like what I need to eat!" snapped the wolf with drool coming down his muzzle.

"Oh good dear, wolf, spare my life!" shrieked and wailed the woman. "I have little children at home. If you eat me, who is to care for them? Don't kill me."

The wolf was puzzled by this. "Now, what am I to do?" His stomach was empty; in fact the woman could hear the wolf's stomach growling. The only problem was that the wolf felt really sorry for the woman and was touched by her pleas.

At last he said, "Go back and live in peace with your children!"

The hungry wolf resumed his efforts to find someone to eat. Around a bend in the trail he saw a sturdy young man. The wolf halted before the young man and said, "I have orders from Heaven to eat you. Be prepared because I will begin at once."

"I must obey if it is so ordered from Heaven. Eat me if that is what you have to do. But before you start, let me measure you to make sure that there is enough room for me in your stomach."

The wolf looked puzzled, "How will you do the measuring?"

"With a proper measuring stick, of course," replied the young man. He went off into the bush beside the trail and cut a good-sized branch from a bush. After he had done this, he took off his belt.

"I have one thing to ask you," said the confused wolf. "What are you going to do with your belt?"

"Oh, this? Here, take it; I present it to you," said the young man. "I am taking it off because it might prevent me from lying comfortably in your stomach." As he said this, the young man tied one end of his belt to the wolf's leg and the other end to the trunk of a big tree.

"Now the measuring begins," the young man announced. And immediately he delivered heavy blows, as fast as hail, upon the wolf's back.

The shocked beast tried to free himself and flee but he could not do so. "Dear friend, do not beat me any longer!" begged the wolf. "I promise not to eat you. I never for even an instant meant to do such a thing!"

"I don't care whether you eat me or not. You will get a good beating from me anyhow," said the young man between whacks. And so the young man measured and measured the wolf's sides until all of the wolf's fur came off. The wolf jerked and jumped about, howling with pain and rage. At last the belt broke and the wolf was able to escape and run off.

When he got back to his fellow wolves in the woods he complained of the terrible luck he had been having. The whole pack of wolves decided to go and punish the insolent young man. And they went as fast as they could.

The young man heard them coming through the brush and knew he was in real danger. Quick as a flash he climbed up a big tree for safety. The pack of angry wolves gathered under the tree and snarled fiercely at the man in the tree. When that didn't do any good, the wolves held a council of war.

The wolf who had been beaten proposed, "Let us all lie down, one upon the other, so that the pile made by our bodies will be high enough for our topmost brother wolf to reach the offender." The whole pack was pleased with this plan. The wolf who had been beaten laid himself down first. The rest climbed one upon another's back, and the heap of wolves grew higher and higher until it was high enough to reach their victim.

"Just you wait, Beaten Sides! I tanned your hide once, and you will get a worse tanning now!" shouted the defiant young man. Hearing these words, the beaten wolf sprang up in terror and fled. The whole pile of wolves tumbled down. Some of them broke their necks, while others broke their legs or ribs. They all ran for their lives and vanished into the woods, just as fast as they could behind Beaten Sides.

The young man came down the tree carefully and continued peacefully on his way. The wolves abandoned forever their thoughts of vengeance against him.

And that is why, ever since that day, the wolf runs away when he meets a man, but the sight of sheep still makes him furious, because the belt the young man beat the wolf with was woven of sheep's wool. ✖

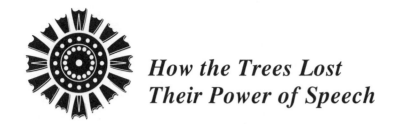

How the Trees Lost Their Power of Speech

Back in the old days when everything was peaceful, a man went into the forest to cut some firewood. He came up to a likely-looking birch tree and got ready to cut it down. Just as he was ready to swing his axe, the birch begged plaintively, "Allow me to live! I am still a young tree and have many children who need me and would mourn my death."

Never before had a tree spoken to the woodcutter. He took pity on the birch tree and went on to an oak tree. Again he was just ready to swing his axe when the oak stopped him in mid-swing. "Let me live! I am still strong and robust. My acorns are unripe and unfit for planting. Where will future generations get oak wood if I and my acorns are to be destroyed?"

Again, the man listened to this argument, so he moved over to an ash tree, which wailed, "Let me live! I am young, I got married only yesterday. What will become of my wife, poor thing, if you kill me now?"

The woodcutter went over to a maple tree, and it too begged, "Let me live! My sap is now flowing, and I have to feed many small creatures with it. What will become of them if you cut me down?"

And so it went with every tree. Each begged the woodcutter for mercy in a human voice. Never could the woodcutter cut these trees down. The aspen tree asked for mercy because, "I was created to rustle my leaves in the wind and to frighten the wrongdoers from their wicked ways."

"I have to give shelter to the singing birds, and the birds would leave the country if I get cut down. The people would be deprived of the beautiful singing of the birds!" said the wild cherry tree.

Even the mountain ash had a reason for why it should not be cut down: "The clusters of my berries are still growing. In order to provide the birds with food during the fall and winter, my berries are needed. What would become of the poor birds if I were hacked down right now?"

"Well," thought the man, "I guess I will chop down the fir trees." But the spruce and the pine he went to next also begged him to spare them, saying, "We have to stay green to adorn nature, especially in winter."

The juniper, of whom it is said that it is the real treasure of the woods and the bringer of happiness to all creatures, animals as well as men, begged especially hard to be spared. "My juice cures ninety-nine diseases. Why would you want to kill me?"

What could the poor compassionate woodcutter do but pass the juniper by? He sat on a hillside in deep meditation. "What will I do now? How dare I go home empty-handed? My wife is waiting for wood to use in the stove for cooking and heating."

As he sat there, troubled, an old man with a long gray beard stepped out of the forest. He wore a shirt of birch bark and a coat of spruce bark. The newcomer walked over to the woodcutter and asked him, "What is troubling you?"

The woodcutter told him his story about how he had found the trees alive and full of their own wishes and their own language. He also told the old man that he couldn't resist their arguments for mercy. The stranger gave him a cheerful look and thanked him for having spared his children and for listening to their requests. As a token of his gratitude, he gave the woodcutter a rod of gold that would fulfill all of his wishes in the future. He also warned the cutter to take care that the wishes should never be extravagant or impossible, or else misfortune would happen instead of happiness.

If the woodcutter wanted to build a building, he had only to go to an anthill, wave the rod three times over it, and explain how the work was to be done. By next morning his orders would be followed. If he needed food, he had only to tell the kettle what he wanted. If he wanted some sweets, he had to show the rod of gold to the bees, and they would bring him more honeycomb than he and his family would ever be able to use.

The trees would give him sap, milk, and healing juice. If he needed silk, linen, or woolen fabrics, spiders would weave just as he desired them.

"I am the spirit of the woods," said the stranger. "I have been assigned to rule over the trees." After he said that, he disappeared.

Back home, the woodcutter's wicked wife met him angrily and insulted him when she saw him returning without the wood. "All the birch twigs should gather into bunches of rods and whip those who are lazy," she told him.

"Let it happen just as you wish," said the woodcutter, waving the rod, and the quarrelsome wife got a good spanking! He was quite pleased when he saw that his golden rod had become a corrector of his bad-tempered wife.

Next, the woodcutter decided to try out the building ability of the ants. He ordered them to build him a new grain storehouse in the backyard. The very next morning it was finished. There was no one happier than the woodcutter. The kettle cooked and served his food. Spiders wove wonderful fabrics. The moles plowed his fields. Ants sowed seeds in the spring and gathered his crops in the fall. He didn't need the help of a human hand any more.

The woodcutter lived happily to the end of his life. He was careful to heed the warning of the wood spirit and never wished for impossible things, nor was he greedy. At his death he left the magic rod to his children. It was also a great blessing for them.

Years later, in the third generation, the rod became the property of a foolish man who disobeyed the orders of his parents and began to demand all kinds of absurd things. He wanted to test the power of the rod, so one day he ordered it to bring the sun down from the heaven to warm his back.

As it was impossible to fulfill this wish, hot rays shot down from the sun. They burned up the offender, his house, and all of his belongings. No trace was left of the place where the foolish man had lived. This was the punishment for his disobedience.

The magic rod was probably melted in the fire, for nobody ever found it. It is believed that the trees in the woods became so frightened by the fire that they lost their power of speech forever. Nobody since that time has heard a word from trees, but they do whisper and whisper among themselves.

Sacks of Cold and Heat

On a gloomy night in the late fall, somebody knocked at the door of a poor peasant. "Kind people, give me lodging for the night," begged the stranger. "I have come from far away and am very tired."

The peasant asked the stranger where he was from, and the stranger replied, "I am the youngest son of Pakkaherra (Jack Frost), the master of the far north where the northern lights continually flame in the skies."

This answer did not satisfy the peasant. "Where are you going, stranger?"

"Where am I going?" repeated the stranger. "I do not know myself. The whole summer I have slept at home because I was angry with the hot sun who bothered me in my work. Now that it is autumn I have a desire to travel and see foreign lands and their peoples. Please let me in. I will be very grateful for lodging. I really am very tired after my long trip."

The peasant allowed him to come in and to spend the night. He told the stranger to climb into the bed shelf above the oven because it was rather chilly in the room. The peasant then went to bed in his bedroom.

The next morning the peasant came into the room where he had left his guest, and the room seemed to be as cold as a cellar. His teeth chattered, so he wrapped himself carefully in his fur coat. He looked around for his guest, and to his amazement, he saw that though the oven was all covered with white frost, his guest was lying on it—bare and uncovered!

Anxiously the peasant called, "Stranger, stranger! Get up! Are you alive or has the cold and frost killed you?" He had to call and call again before finally the stranger woke up.

The stranger stretched and yawned. "The room was so hot that I could not even close my eyes during the night. It was only when it was close to dawn that I got a little sleep."

"The room too hot?" exclaimed the peasant. "The room is so cold that it makes my teeth chatter."

Thanking his host for his hospitality and lodging, the stranger went on his way. The peasant was really curious as to who the stranger could be. Outside, everything was covered with a hard frost.

Several weeks went by. Another stranger was passing the peasant's hut, and he also begged for a night's lodging. "I am the second son of Pakkaherra, the master of the far north, the land where the northern lights flame across the skies."

"You must be the brother of the fellow who stayed here recently. In fact, the night he was here was when we had our first frost of the year," said the peasant. "Where are you going?"

"You ask me where I am going? I do not know myself. The whole summer I have slept at home and was angry with the hot sun because he would not let me do anything. Now that winter is almost here, a longing arose in me to travel and visit foreign lands and foreign peoples. Please take me in for the night, and I will be very thankful."

Just as before, the second stranger went to sleep in the bed shelf above the oven, and, as usual, the peasant went into the other room. On the following morning it was so cold in the room that the logs in the wall cracked and the water was frozen in the barrel. The stove was covered with a deeper white frost than before. Nevertheless, the guest was uncovered and soundly sleeping.

The peasant worried that the stranger might be frozen to death and did not even try to wake him up, but went beside him and touched him to make sure he was dead. To the peasant's shock, the stranger sprang up at once and began to rub his eyes.

"It was so hot here last night," he said. "I could not even fall asleep until it was dawn. Then I was able to close my eyes and sleep. That is why you found me sleeping so late this morning."

The peasant wondered, "Still hot! It is so cold in here that the water is frozen and has broken my water barrel. What an unusual man you are to complain of the heat while it is so cold. Not only that, you slept uncovered above the oven!"

"I told you I was the son of Pakkaherra," said the traveler. "Thank you very much for letting me stay with you." With that the stranger went on his way.

A few weeks later, a third stranger passed along the same road and he too came to the peasant's hut to ask for permission to stay overnight. The peasant asked him, "Who are you and where are you going?"

"Do you want to know who I am and where I am going?" the stranger asked. "I am neither of noble birth nor of humble birth. I am the eldest son of Pakkaherra, the master of the far north. Because of heavy heat I had to sleep the whole summer. Now I want to go further to visit other lands and nations."

"So you are the oldest son of Pakkaherra?" exclaimed the peasant. "Then, go away if that is who you are! For such men as are in your family I have no place. I know your kind. Your two brothers have been here and have done much harm to me. They promised to be grateful, but they were merely biting their thumbs at me. Neither mouth nor eye received anything from them. I am sure you will be no better than your brothers before you. Therefore, go away!"

The stranger pleaded and begged and coaxed to be taken in.

"You want to stay overnight in order to cause me more frost damage," scolded the peasant.

"Dear friend, forgive me if my younger brothers have harmed you. Also, please forgive me if they forgot to be grateful. I however, will be really thankful. If you do not want to let me into your room, allow me to go into the loft. I will be content with that."

The peasant thought and thought before he answered the stranger, "Well, if you go up to the loft and will be satisfied to stay there, then you may stay overnight."

The son of Pakkaherra climbed up to the loft, and the peasant went into his bedroom. In the morning when the peasant woke up, the trees were all covered with ice and were snapping with frost. Outdoors it was so cold that it hurt his teeth. The door to the loft, however, stood wide open. He could see the stranger lying there uncovered.

The crunching of the frost under the peasant's footsteps woke the stranger. "It was quite pleasant to sleep here. The weather was so nice and cool that I was able to sleep even without eating."

The surprised peasant asked, "So, so! Was it not cold?"

"Ha! This cold is nothing. You should see my father! Then you would sing a song about the frost. Wherever he goes it is so cold that the birds fall dead even as they are flying. During the summer, my father flees from his home to find shelter in the place where earth and the skies meet each other. In winter Pakkaherra likes to sit at home. He is quite content there and does not care to leave home."

The son of Pakkaherra was ready to go, and he started off. Suddenly he stopped. "Is that not strange? I came near to forgetting to thank you as my brothers did."

He opened his pack and took out of it two small sacks and gave them to the peasant. "These two sacks will be your reward for having received the three of us so kindly. The white sack is the cold sack, and the black sack is the heat sack. If you need cold or heat, open the mouth of the sack a little bit. If you open the sack entirely, either biting cold or suffocating heat will rush out." With that, the stranger went on his way.

The peasant was eager to try out the sacks. He went into his hut and opened the black sack a little. At once it was hot in the room. It was as if the stove had been red hot. The peasant had to take off his fur coat it was so hot.

The peasant took his heat sack outdoors early in the spring, and at once the snow melted quickly. Everything began to grow and turn green.

Once each day he went out and opened his heat sack, and the frost never harmed his small fields again. His crops grew better than ever before.

Now that he had the two sacks, life became easy for the peasant. The heat sack heated his hut nicely, and there was no more need to cut firewood! People in the village became curious to know why the spring arrived earlier at the hut of the peasant than at their places. Why was it always so warm there? No matter how often the villagers asked him, the peasant would not tell them his secret. Somehow, though, the people found out that the peasant owned a special heat sack. Rumors of it reached the ears of the rich farmer who owned the land where the peasant lived. The rich master asked the poor man, "Is it true that you possess a special heat sack?"

"Yes, it is true, master," replied the peasant.

"You do not need such a thing. Give me the sack. Go bring it right now!" ordered the landowner.

Reluctantly the peasant went home, but he had no intention of giving away his precious sack. It was winter, and the landowner wanted winter gone.

"It is time to punish the wretched fellow for not obeying my order," thought the landowner. He went out to the hut of the peasant. "Get out of that hut! It belongs to me," he yelled to the peasant.

"Wait just a moment, honorable master," replied the peasant. He brought out his cold sack and opened it on the threshold. Immediately it became unbearably cold. The landowner was forced to hurry away to save himself from freezing. After that, he never dared try to make the peasant move out of his hut.

The very richest farmer in the village heard stories about the magic heat sack. He came to the peasant's hut to bargain for the sack. "I will give you as much gold as the sack will hold," promised the rich farmer.

"Keep your gold. What can I, a poor man, do with the gold? The gold will not heat my room. Keep your gold and I will happily keep my sack," said the peasant.

Have you ever seen a rich man when he became really angry because he couldn't get what he wanted? He was furious. That night the rich man came back and stole the peasant's heat sack. Now he was pleased with his success. At his home, the rich man opened the sack wide. Scorching heat puffed into his face, and it became as hot in the house as if it were a kiln. Everyone hurried to get out of the house. Some of them had burned noses, some burned hands, and others had their faces burned. Even the animals that were under the same roof in the stable were burned to death. Nobody was able to reach the wretched animals and let them loose.

Probably, worse than the calamity that had befallen the rich farmer was bearing the name of being a thief because everyone knew he had stolen the sack. Nobody dared to enter his house because they would also get burned. There was nothing left for the rich farmer to do but to go to the peasant and confess his sin. He would ask his forgiveness and beg for the peasant's help.

The peasant forgave him and helped him willingly. He took his cold sack and went with the rich farmer. He only had to open his cold sack to make the unbearable heat cool down. Then the peasant got his heat sack back. The farmer was happy too because he could again enter his house.

After a while, the king of the land heard stories about the unique sacks. The king offered the peasant gold and silver, but the poor man didn't want either of those things. Then the king got a clever thought. He invited the peasant to bring his sacks and come live with him in his palace.

With these new events, the peasant became an important person. He ate and drank at the king's table and wore rich clothes provided by the king. In return for this he only had to open the heat sack once a day in the palace and the palace gardens. That way it was always warm in the palace, and the trees and bushes in the gardens bloomed all the year just as they used to bloom on St. John's day.

A messenger brought news to the king that there was an enemy in the land. The king sent out a large army against the foe, but the army was beaten. Then the king sent his very bravest men with an even larger army, but it met the same miserable fate. The enemy had now moved near the royal city. The king told the peasant of his alarm and distress.

"Do not be afraid," said the peasant. "Let the enemies come. Open wide the gates of the city, and then you and your people go and hide somewhere. I will meet the enemy."

The king did as he was told and ordered all the population of the city to gather in an underground refuge that had been dug in case of severe need. Then the locks were removed from the gates, and the enemy was able to enter the city without any trouble.

With shouts of joy, the enemy appeared before the city and passed through the gates. To their surprise, they did not find a human being in the whole city. They searched and searched, but all of the city people had vanished.

The victorious enemy began to celebrate. They gorged on food and caroused. At last, worn out by excessive rejoicing and feasting, they all fell asleep. The peasant had secretly watched all of this. When they were fast asleep, the peasant said to himself, "Now is the time!"

He opened his cold sack and threw it into the city. After that, he joined the king and his people in the safe hiding place and closed the entrances to the underground passages.

The next morning some of the city people ventured out of their hiding places to see what had happened in the city. Scarcely had they poked their heads out when a chill blew into their faces and they had to retreat.

The peasant came to their aid and opened his heat sack a little. The cold instantly left. He hurried to the cold sack and closed it. All the people came out of hiding and went into the city to see what the enemy was doing. They looked and looked and at last saw all of the enemy soldiers lying on the ground, dead. There was one here, another there, some another place, and they were all frozen. The city people went into their houses. Everywhere they went they found their dead enemies.

Since that time no enemy has dared to attack that kingdom. The king and the peasant lived happily together to the end of their lives. After their deaths, the cold and heat sacks disappeared, and nobody has seen them since. ✖

The Cat and Mouse

Ages ago there was a cat and a mouse who were friends. "Let's gather our winter supplies," suggested the cat. The cat, being wealthier and quicker of wit, got an earthen pot. The mouse began to store up fat in the pot.

Soon the pot was filled. A dog, however, had smelled the fat in the air and began to sniff around for the fat pot.

The mouse said to the cat, "My friend, our fat pot is in danger. We must take it to a safer place."

"Very good, my friend. The dog is after it and getting closer," replied the cat. They carried the fat pot to the church and hid it in the basement under the altar. The following Sunday the cat said, "Today I have been asked to stand sponsor at a christening, and so I must go to church."

"Go if you must, but do not forget to have a look at our fat pot," advised the mouse. Later in the evening the mouse asked the name of the cat's godchild.

"A Little Off," was the answer.

"That is a peculiar name. Never in my life have I heard anything like that," squeaked the mouse.

The following Sunday the cat went again to the church to stand sponsor at another christening. "What name was given to this godchild?" questioned the mouse when the cat returned from church.

"Half Gone," the cat replied.

On the third Sunday the same thing happened. This time the godchild's name was "Some Left." On the fourth Sunday it was "Bottom Bare."

"Aha, friend, now I know what you meant by those names," cried the mouse. "The first time you ate a little of the fat, then a half, then some was still left, and at last all the fat was gone. You emptied our fat pot, old friend! You are a deceiver and a thief!"

"How dare you insult me," screamed the cat. "You wretched creature!" In an instant the cat caught the mouse and ate it without pity. From that time on, no mouse has ever sought the friendship of a cat.

The Master of the Gold

On a night between Christmas and New Year's, there was a heavy storm. A traveler lost his way and became almost exhausted as he pushed ahead through the deep snow drifts. He thanked his luck, though, when he found shelter from the storm under a large juniper bush.

He planned to stay there overnight and find his way in the morning. Wrapping himself like a hedgehog in his fur coat, he soon fell asleep. He did not know how long he had been asleep when he felt somebody shaking him.

"Stranger, get up!" The snowstorm will bury you and you might never get out," a voice called.

The traveler raised his head, opened his sleepy eyes, and saw before him a tall man with a young pine tree twice his size as a staff in his hand. "Come with me," said the man. "We have a warm bonfire in the woods. It will be better to rest there than here in the open."

How could the traveler refuse such a gracious invitation? He got up and went with the man. The snowstorm was so furious that it was impossible to see more than three paces ahead, but when the man with the pine tree staff raised his staff and called, "Stop there, mother of the snowstorm. Give way," there at once appeared in front of them a quiet wide roadway. No snow fell on the roadway while on both sides of them the angry snow raged. It seemed as if an invisible wall was holding back the snow.

After quite some time the men reached the woods. From far off they could see the glow of the fire. "What is your name?" the man with the pine tree staff asked the traveler.

"Juhanni," was the answer.

Three men sat around the fire. They were dressed in white linen clothes as if it were midsummer. Thirty or more steps from the fire it looked as if it really were summer. The moss was dry, and green leaves and plants were growing. Ants and bugs roamed on the lawn. At the same time Juhanni could hear the roaring of the storm and the falling of the snow. More strange was the fire itself. It shone very brightly but did not give off any smoke.

"Do you think, Juhanni, that this is a better place to rest than under the juniper bush in the open?" said the man with the pine tree staff.

Juhanni had to agree that it really was better by the fire and thanked his guide for bringing him to this place. Then he took off his fur coat, rolled it up and put it as a pillow under his head, and laid himself down by the fire.

The man with the pine tree staff got his flask from under a tree and offered Juhanni a drink. The drink was unusually good and made Juhanni feel happy. The man with the pine tree staff also laid down. Juhanni did not understand the language in which the man and his three companions talked, and soon he fell asleep.

When Juhanni awoke the next morning he found himself in an unknown place. He could not see either woods or fire. Rubbing his eyes and remembering what he had seen the night before, Juhanni figured that it must all have been a dream. There was only one problem—he could not explain to himself how he got here.

Juhanni felt the ground under him trembling and heard a heavy noise from afar. He listened for a while in the direction from which the noise came and decided to see what it was. He hoped he would find some people there.

Soon he came to the entrance of a cave from which came the noise. Light glowed feebly from the cave. Juhanni entered and found himself in an immense blacksmith shop with many bellows and anvils. Seven work-men were at each anvil. These blacksmiths were not like ordinary people. They were about knee-high, and their heads were larger than their bodies. The hammers they held in their hands were twice as big as they were. With these hammers the little fellows struck heavy blows on the anvils. Their blows were more powerful than those of full-size men. The little black-smiths had nothing on except long leather aprons that covered their fronts. Their backs were as naked as Mother Nature had made them.

Juhanni noticed the man with the pine tree staff near the back wall. He was sitting on a tall tree trunk and watching the work of the little men very carefully. At his feet stood a wooden pan from which the little workers drank from time to time.

The man with the pine tree staff turned out to be the master of the blacksmiths. He wasn't wearing the white clothes he had worn the night before but had on dark, dust-covered clothes. He wore a leather girdle with a huge clasp. The pine tree staff was still in his hand, and with it he made signs to his men now and then, because there was such loud noise and constant vibration that no talk could be heard. Juhanni didn't know if anybody had noticed him because the master and his men were all working hard.

Some hours later the little men got to rest. The bellows stopped, and the heavy hammers were thrown down. When the workers were gone, the master arose from his seat and motioned Juhanni to come nearer.

"I saw you coming," he remarked. "Our hasty work did not permit me to talk to you earlier. Be my guest today. You will see my life and my household. Entertain yourself while I change my working clothes."

The master took a key from his pocket and opened a door in the back wall. He invited Juhanni to enter. In the room, Juhanni saw a storehouse of marvelous treasures. There were mountains of gold and silver bars piled everywhere. Juhanni began to count the bars of gold in one of the piles. He had counted exactly five hundred and seventy bars when the master returned and said with a smile, "Stop counting. It will take too much time. Better take a few bars from the pile. I want to present them to you."

Juhanni did not need to be asked twice. He grasped a bar of gold in each hand, but he could not even move them.

"You feeble flea," laughed the master. "You cannot take with you even the smallest gift I offer. Therefore you have to be satisfied with only looking at it." The master led Juhanni to more rooms until they reached a seventh room, which was the size of a church. Like all the others, it was stored from floor to ceiling with gold and silver bars.

Juhanni was amazed by the endless treasure. There was so much here that you could buy all the kingdoms of the world with it. What was it all doing here unused? He asked his host, "Why are you storing these fortunes here? Nobody can profit from them just sitting here. If you plan to divide them among the people of the world, all men would be rich. There would be no need for anyone in the world to work again."

The master answered him, "That is why I cannot give these treasures to mankind. All the world would perish with idleness. If people had no need to work they would soon die. People are intended to toil in order to feed themselves."

Juhanni did not agree with this reasoning. He argued boldly for the master to explain what use was all the gold and silver stored there only to tarnish. He also asked, "Why do you tirelessly store more and more treasure even though you have more than enough?"

"I am not a man even though I have the figure of a human and a human face," the gold master answered. "I am a higher being who has been assigned to rule the world and keep order in it. My helpers and I have to make gold and silver here underground. Every year a small portion of it is given out for people to use. They get exactly as much as they need for their use. We break the gold into small pieces and mix it with soil, clay, and sand. Men have to find it by chance, and they must dig for it with much work. It is now mealtime, so we must bring this talk to an end. If you still want to look at my treasures, stay here. Delight your heart with the sight of the glittering gold and the shining silver. I will come to take you to the table." With that, he left Juhanni alone.

Juhanni walked from room to room. He tried to lift some smaller bars of gold, but again he could not even budge them. He had often heard from others that gold was heavy, but he never believed that it could be this heavy.

When the master of the gold returned, he was so transformed that at first Juhanni did not recognize him. He wore a bright, flame-colored, silken garment richly adorned with gold. Around his waist was a palm-wide golden belt. On his head he had a glittering golden crown with precious stones sparkling in it like the stars in a winter sky. Instead of his former pine tree staff, he held in his hand a small wand of purest gold that bore branches and pine needles. It looked like a child of the big pine tree staff.

The master of all this royal wealth closed and locked the doors of the gold chambers. He put the keys into his pocket, took Juhanni by the hand, and led him out of the smithy into another room. A fine meal was served to them there. All the tables and the chairs were silver. In the middle of the room stood a grand table with silver chairs on opposite sides. The plates, pitchers, cups, and glasses were golden.

The two men seated themselves at the table, and twelve gourmet dishes of food were served. The servants looked like the little blacksmiths Juhanni had seen earlier. This time they were dressed in white clothes, not naked as when they were blacksmiths.

Juhanni was amazed by the swiftness and skill of the little men. The quickness of their movements was almost like flying even though they did not have wings. They were not as tall as the table so they had to jump on it regularly, like fleas. Even though they jumped, they carried big plates and dishes brimming with food with such skill that not one drop was spilled. Between courses, they filled the cups of the master and Juhanni with mead and rare wines.

The master and Juhanni talked in a warm manner, and the master told Juhanni some secrets. He said, "Between Christmas and New Year's I often wander on the Earth. I wish to become acquainted with some human beings to see how they live. From what I have learned about men, I cannot praise them much. Most of them seem to be living to spite and harm each other. They are always complaining about someone else, and they never see their own faults. They blame someone else for any misfortunes they have."

Juhanni tried to deny this as well as he could as the hospitable master of the gold ordered the servants to pour more and more of the delicious wine into Juhanni's cup. Juhanni's tongue became heavy and didn't seem to work right. At last Juhanni could not understand what was being said to him.

He fell asleep and had a strange dream in which piles of gold were constantly before his eyes. In this dream he was much stronger and could easily carry a pair of gold bars. However, he seemed to get tired and needed to sit down and rest. He heard strange voices that he thought were those of the blacksmiths.

Half opening his eyes, he saw a green forest around him and grass under him. The sun was shining brightly and threw its warm rays into his eyes. It took some time for Juhanni to free himself from the bonds of sleep and to recall what had happened to him. By and by his memory returned, but everything he remembered seemed strange and did not agree with the world as he knew it. It seemed that all his adventures with the man with the pine tree staff had happened only a few days ago. But here it was not winter; full summer was around him. Had he been under some mysterious charm?

Juhanni rose from the ground and saw the place where the bonfire had been. The cinders glittered in the sun in an unusual way. He examined the place more closely and saw that the supposed ash heap was of fine silver dust, and there were bars of pure gold. What luck! Juhanni wondered where he would get a bag to take it all home. Need is the best teacher; Juhanni took off his winter fur coat and swept all the silver ashes into it, being careful not to ignore a single grain of dust. He put all the gold bars on his fur coat, made it into a bundle, and fastened it with his belt so nothing could fall out. The load did not look large, but it was heavy, and Juhanni had to use all his strength to carry it to a safe place and hide it.

Juhanni became a rich man and was able to buy himself an estate. He decided to leave this part of the country and move to another place. There, in the new land, he bought a beautiful manor house and married a lovely maiden. They lived happily until the end of their lives. ✠

Witch Trial of Jarmo Kivimaki on May 9, 1627

The court bailiff called Jarmo Kivimaki to the stand and asked Jarmo what he did the time he made sailing wind for a friend who had come to him two years before.

"My friend wanted a sailing wind for a trip he was taking to Sweden across the Gulf of Bothnia. No money exchanged hands for producing this sailing wind since my friend promised to pay me when he returned," answered Jarmo.

He told the court that, "I took off my right shoe, and washed my bare foot in the sea while the water was quiet and commanded, 'Wind to land! Wind to land!' The favorable sailing wind came, and I asked those sailing not to set too much sail until they passed the islands. After that they could set as much sail as the boat would tolerate."

"The Saturday before All Saints' Day, my friend's wife came to me and asked me to make a sailing wind so her husband could come home soon. She promised to give me a jug of beer for my trouble. I told her I would, and with that, I took a young pig and threw it into the sea and commanded: 'Wind to sea! Wind to sea!'"

"The pig squirmed too much in the sun, and the wind became too strong. Then I told the wife, 'God have mercy on them! I am afraid that they have taken off too early and that the wind is too strong. If they took off at the beginning of the storm, may God have mercy, or they will not return.' None of the sailors on that ship made it home."

The bailiff asked Jarmo if he had made sailing wind other times.

"Yes, I have often made wind for people and a quarter of a year ago I made wind for a ship because they requested that I do so. So I washed my foot, as I said before, and got a gentle southern wind."

The next question from the bailiff was, "Do you know how to do sorcery?"

"Yes," replied Jarmo. "I am a rune singer or *tietaja* (man of knowledge, or sage), but I never take anything for my runic spells."

"What are runic spells?" asked the bailiff.

Jarmo began, "When one wants to cast rune spells, one takes a rune drum. It is called a *kannus* and can be made of fir, pine or birch. The Tree of Life is painted there and rules all four directions of the universe. A *lovi* or hole is painted in the center of the drum and leads from one level of the universe to another. As a *tietaja* I can travel to the underworld or to the upper spirit world.

"I also paint all kinds of animals on the drum that can bring luck. I then beat the drum with a horn hammer lined with beaver skin. While I beat the drum I chant the runic songs until I have traveled to the other world. The copper piece hops around on the drum and finally stops on one of the lines. From that I know what will happen in the future.

"People come to me when they want help to heal someone who is sick or whose soul needs help."

The court bailiff asked Jarmo how he learned these things.

"I was first introduced to the ritual when I was just a small boy. The status of sage is given to the person who knows the myths, stories, and songs the best. These stories became part of the cure for illness and the restoration of health. I have known great sages who were able to chant as many as fourteen or fifteen generations of their wise predecessors." Jarmo continued, "Once many magicians came together to beat the drum to see whose art was strongest."

The next question from the bailiff was, "Who taught you to control the wind?"

"A great Finn rune singer who is now dead. He taught me before the time of the war," answered Jarmo.

The records show that at the following court session Jarmo Kivimaki was condemned to death by fire and stake along with his magical drum. ⊠

Part III

Recipes

6

Favorite Finnish Recipes

Main Dishes

Pannukakku *or Finnish* **P**ancakes

4 eggs	½ cup sugar
2 cups milk	1 cup flour
½ teaspoon salt	

Beat eggs with 1 cup of milk until well blended. Stir in salt, sugar, and flour to make a smooth batter. Stir in remainder of milk. Set batter aside for 10 minutes.

Butter a 12" x 8" x 2" baking dish. Stir batter and pour into pan. Bake in hot oven (400 degrees) for 30 minutes or until pancake is golden brown and puffy. Serve immediately with jam. (Variations can include serving it with cinnamon sugar and maple syrup for breakfast.)

Lihäpyörykät *or Finnish* Meatballs

3/4 cup soft bread crumbs
1 cup light cream or milk
1½ pounds lean ground beef
1 onion, minced
1 slightly beaten egg

1½ teaspoons salt
½ teaspoon ground allspice
2 tablespoons butter for frying
2 tablespoons flour
1½ cup milk

Soak the crumbs in ½ cup of the cream. Mix in the beef, onion, egg, salt, and allspice. Shape into balls. Melt the butter in a frying pan and brown the meatballs a few at a time. Turn the meatballs so they brown evenly. After all the meat is browned, remove from the pan. Add flour to the pan drippings, stir, and brown over medium heat. Slowly add the second ½ cup of cream and the milk. Stir to smooth the ingredients. Add water if necessary to thin out the gravy. Return the meatballs to the pan, cover, and simmer over low heat for 25 minutes.

Kalakukko *or Fish* Loaf

One of the most traditional dishes of Kuopio, in the Lake District, is kalakukko. When we visited there Cousin Liisa promised us a treat. There is a bakery in Kuopio that makes and ships them throughout Finland. We went to the market square and bought several of these for a picnic. Kalakukko is made of salt pork, perch, and whitefish cooked in a heavy rye crust for several hours at low heat. The kukko bakes so long that the bones of the fish melt.

Crust

1 package of dry yeast
1 cup warm water
1 teaspoon salt

4 tablespoons soft butter
1½ cup rye flour
1½ cup white flour

Filling

1 pound small fish (2 to 3
    medium-sized trout or about
    14 smelts)
1 teaspoon salt

dash pepper
4 slices salt pork or bacon, cut
    into 1" pieces

Dissolve the yeast in the warm water. Add the salt and butter. Stir in the rye and white flour slowly, until the ingredients are well mixed and form a stiff dough. Knead lightly on a floured board until smooth. Replace the dough in the bowl, cover, and let rise until doubled in size. Pour the dough onto the floured board and shape into an oval about ½" thick, 12" long, and 10" wide.

Rub the surface of the pastry with flour to dry it. Clean the fish (remove heads and tails). Dry fish thoroughly and arrange on the dough side-by-side or in layers. Sprinkle with salt and pepper and top with the pork. Smooth the dough up over the mound of fish to cover it completely. Dampen the outside of the dough with water to seal the edges and smooth the top. If the dough cracks, moisten the broken edge and reseal. The dough should now have the shape of a loaf of bread.

Place in a well-buttered casserole dish, add 2 tablespoons of water to the dish, and cover the dish. Bake at 300 degrees for 4 hours. After the first hour of baking, brush the surface of the loaf with melted butter. After the third hour, remove the cover, remove the kukko from the oven, and wrap it in foil. Return it to the casserole to bake for another hour. Let it cool wrapped in the foil to soften the crust. Slice it crosswise to serve. (Serves 6)

Lohikeitto *or Salmon* Stew

Fish in all forms is used for many purposes in Finland. Fresh salmon is versatile and is even used in stew.

1 pound cleaned salmon	3 to 4 medium potatoes, peeled
2 teaspoons salt	and diced
1 medium onion, chopped	2 cups milk
½ teaspoon dill weed	2 to 3 tablespoons butter
4 cups water	chives or fresh dill

Cut the fish into 2" pieces. Place the fish, salt, onion, and dill weed in a large pot and cover with the water. Bring to the boiling point and simmer until the fish flakes when pierced with a fork. Drain, but save the liquid to use as stock for boiling the potatoes.

Put the potatoes in a saucepan, add the fish stock, and cook until the potatoes are tender. Pour the potatoes and liquid back into the pan with the cooked salmon and add the milk. Simmer slowly for about 20 minutes. Garnish with cut chives or fresh dill. (Serves about 6)

Omenasilli *or Herring in Sour* Cream

1½ to 2 cups herring fillets,
    sliced crosswise
1 medium-sized red onion, thinly
    sliced and separated into rings
1 large tart apple, grated

2 cups sour cream
1 teaspoon dry mustard
½ teaspoon sugar
1 bunch chopped green onions

Mix all the ingredients except the green onions. Cover and chill at least 2 hours before serving. Garnish with chopped green onions.

Keitetty Lipeäkala *or* Lutefisk

This is a special dish for the Christmas season. When Norma J. Livo first saw it seasoning in the basement washtubs she was skeptical, but it all turned into a new treat.

Buy 2 pounds of commercial lutefisk. (The old way to make it was to soak a large dried codfish in water for a week. Change the water daily. Then soak the fish for 3 to 5 days—until the meat is shiny—in a strong solution of raw soda and ashes mixed with water. The ashes provided lye to dissolve the fish bones. Then soak the fish for 7 more days in fresh water, changing the water daily. This removed the lye.)

2 quarts water
2 tablespoons salt
ground allspice

white sauce (your favorite recipe)
melted butter

Cut the fish into large pieces and tie in a cheesecloth or clean towel. Pour the water into a large pot (do not use an aluminum pan). Add the salt and bring to a boil. Put the fish bundle into the water and simmer for about 10 minutes. Remove the fish to a serving platter (avoid metal platters). Sprinkle the fish with allspice and serve covered with white sauce and melted butter.

Hernekeitto *or Pea* Soup

2 cups whole dried yellow peas
   or 1 cup whole dried yellow
   peas and 1 cup split yellow
   peas
6 whole allspice
2 cups cubed ham or a ham bone
   that has meat on it
2 quarts water

1 cup diced carrots
½ cup diced onion
2 cups diced potatoes
1 teaspoon salt
dash of pepper

Rinse whole peas and cover with water. Soak overnight. (The split peas do not need to be soaked.) Next day, drain the peas. Simmer the peas, allspice, and ham in 2 quarts of water for 1 hour or until the skins pop on the peas. If using a ham bone, remove the bone and scrape the meat into the soup. Add carrots, onion, potatoes, salt, and pepper. Simmer over low heat for 1 hour. Makes 3 quarts soup.

Punajuurisalaatti *or Beet* Salad

1 tablespoon vinegar
¼ cup heavy cream
½ cup mayonnaise

1½ teaspoon horseradish
pinch of salt
2 cups cooked beets, diced

Mix together vinegar, cream, mayonnaise, horseradish, and salt. Blend dressing with the beets. Chill. Makes enough for 4 servings.

Lanttulaatikko *or Rutabaga* Casserole

2 medium rutabagas, peeled
   and diced
½ cup fine dry bread crumbs
¼ cup cream
½ teaspoon nutmeg

¼ teaspoon white pepper or
   allspice
1 teaspoon salt
2 eggs, beaten
brown sugar to taste (optional)
3 tablespoons butter

Cook the rutabagas until soft in enough salted water to cover them. Drain and mash the rutabagas. Soak the bread crumbs in the cream and stir in the nutmeg, salt, beaten eggs, white pepper or allspice, and brown sugar. Combine with the mashed rutabagas. Turn mixture into a buttered 2½ quart casserole and dot top with butter. Bake at 350 degrees until lightly browned on top (about 1 hour).

Pulla *or Sweet Braided Yeast* Bread
(Cardamom-flavored)

The Finns are avid coffee drinkers and guests who are warmly welcomed are usually offered coffee. These coffee sessions would not be complete without pulla. Pulla dough is also used to make cinnamon rolls, tea rings, and fruit pies filled with whatever is the fruit of the season—rhubarb in the spring; strawberries, raspberries, bilberries or cloudberries in the summer; and lingonberries or apples in the autumn.

Carefully follow the order of combining ingredients. The melted butter is added after about half of the flour.

1 package dry yeast	7-8 whole cardamom pods, seeded
½ cup warm water	and crushed (about 1 teaspoon)
2 cups milk, scalded and cooled	4 eggs, beaten
to lukewarm	8-9 cups sifted white flour
1 cup sugar (less if desired)	½ cup melted butter
1 teaspoon salt	

Glaze
1 egg, beaten
½ cup chopped or sliced almonds
½ cup granulated sugar

Dissolve the yeast in the warm water. Stir in the milk, sugar, salt, cardamom, eggs, and enough flour to make a batter (about 2 cups flour). Beat until the dough is smooth and elastic. Add 3 cups flour and beat well. The dough should be quite smooth and glossy in appearance. Add the melted butter and stir in well. Beat again until the dough looks glossy again. Stir in the remaining flour until a stiff dough forms.

Lightly flour a board. Place the dough on it and cover with an inverted mixing bowl. Let the dough rest 15 minutes. Knead again until smooth and glossy. Place in a lightly greased mixing bowl. Turn the dough to grease the top. Cover lightly and let rise in a warm place until doubled in size (about 1 hour). Punch down and let rise again until almost doubled (about ½ hour).

Again, place the dough on a slightly floured board. Divide into 9 parts. Shape each part into a strip about 16" long by rolling the dough between your palms and the board. Braid 3 strips together into a straight loaf. Pinch the ends together and tuck them under. Repeat for the other 2 loaves. Put the braids on lightly greased baking sheets. Let rise for about 20 minutes (the braids should be puffy but not doubled in size).

Brush the loaves with the beaten eggs and, if you wish, sprinkle with the sugar and almonds. Bake in a hot oven at 400 degrees for 25 to 30 minutes. Be careful not to overbake or the loaves will be too dry. Remove from the oven when they are a light golden brown. Slice to serve.

Hiivaleipä *or Rye* Bread

1 package dry yeast	¼ cup butter or margarine
½ cup warm water	3 cups medium rye flour
1½ cup hot water	2 cups all-purpose flour
2 tablespoons honey	melted butter
2 teaspoons salt	

In a small bowl, dissolve the yeast in the warm water. In a large bowl, combine the hot water, honey, salt, and butter. Cool to lukewarm. Add yeast mixture and rye flour. Beat with a wooden spoon until smooth. Work in the all-purpose flour (add more if necessary to make a soft dough). Knead until smooth and elastic (about 10 minutes). Put into a warm, greased bowl, turning the dough to grease it all around. Place in a warm place to rise until doubled (about 1 hour). Punch down and let rest 10 minutes. Form into two loaves and place in well-greased 9" x 5" loaf pans. Cover and let rise until doubled (about 45 minutes). Bake at 400 degrees about 30 minutes or until brown on top and loaf sounds hollow when tapped on the bottom. Brush the top with melted butter.

Rieska or Flat Barley Bread

3 cups all-purpose flour
1¾ cups barley or graham flour
1 tablespoon sugar
1 tablespoon baking powder

1 teaspoon baking soda
2 teaspoons salt
½ cup shortening
2 cups buttermilk

Combine the dry ingredients except for the salt. Cut the shortening into dry ingredients with a pastry blender until mixture resembles coarse crumbs. Blend buttermilk and salt and stir into the dry ingredients until a soft dough forms. Pat into a greased 14" x 17" cookie sheet to about ½" thickness. Bake at 425 degrees for 20 minutes or until slightly brown. Makes 1 flat loaf.

Desserts

Riisipuuro or Creamy Oven Rice Pudding

¾ cup white long-grained rice
1 quart whole milk

½ to 1 teaspoon salt
1 tablespoon sugar

Put rice into a 1½ quart baking dish. Cover with milk. Add the salt and sugar. Cover and bake at 350 degrees for about 1 hour or until rice is tender. Do not stir more than 3 times during the baking. If rice starts to dry out during baking, add a little more milk to keep it creamy. Serve with a berry sauce or fruit soup spooned over the top. Makes 6 servings.

Joulutortut or Christmas Prune Tarts

Pastry
4 cups all-purpose flour
1 pound butter
3/4 cup cold water
Filling
1 pound pitted, stewed prunes
½ cup sugar

Cut ½ pound of the butter into the flour until mixture resembles coarse crumbs. Add the water. Chill for 30 minutes.

Roll out the dough and dot with the remaining ½ pound butter. Fold dough from front toward back, from back to front, and from each side toward center. Chill. Repeat the process of rolling and chilling, adding dots of butter, for 3 times or until all the butter is gone. Roll again. Cut in 3" squares. Slit each corner of each square.

Mix the stewed prunes and sugar. Place a spoonful of prune filling in the center of each square. Turn up alternating corners (as in making a pinwheel) and pinch together in the center. Chill. Bake in 400 degree oven for 13 to 15 minutes until golden. Cool on brown paper.

Ässät *or Finnish "S"* Cookies

½ cup softened butter	1½ to 1¾ cups all-purpose flour
¼ cup sugar	1 egg, beaten
1 egg	enough sugar to sprinkle on work
½ teaspoon almond extract	surface to roll the dough and
dash salt	cover with sugar
¼ cup finely chopped toasted almonds	

In a large mixing bowl, cream the butter, sugar, egg, almond extract, and salt until light and fluffy. Stir in enough flour to make dough easy to handle. Blend with hands until smooth.

Shape dough into long strands, ½" thick. Cut into 2½" lengths. Dip into beaten egg. Roll in the sugar. Roll in the almonds. Arrange "S" shapes on greased baking sheets. Bake at 375 degrees until golden (about 8 minutes). Cool on wire racks. Makes 3½ dozen.

Talouskalja *or Home* Beer

A popular summertime nonalcoholic drink served with meals.

1 cup sugar	4 quarts water
1 tablespoon malt extract	1 teaspoon dry yeast

Mix the sugar, malt, and water and bring to the boiling point. Cool. When lukewarm, add the yeast. Stir until it is dissolved. In a nonmetallic container, let the beer stand overnight to ferment. Place into gallon jugs or other bottles to store in the refrigerator or another cool spot. Cap these bottles tightly.

Berries

Finns use fresh berries in desserts, as a fruit soup, as decoration on whipped cream and coffee cakes, as preserves, and as liqueurs. Raspberries, blueberries, gooseberries, bilberries, strawberries, lingonberries, and the exotic golden cloudberries are part of the gourmet riches found in gardens, the marketplaces, and nature.

Color Plates

The Vengeance of Joukahainen, 1897. © Akseli Gallen-Kallela (1865/1931). Tempera on canvas, 125x130 cm. Turku Art Museum, Finland. Photograph: Kari Lehtinen.

The Defence of the Sampo, 1896. © Akseli Gallen-Kallela
(1865/1931). Tempera on canvas, 122x125 cm.
Turku Art Museum, Finland. Photograph: Kari Lehtinen.

Lemminkäinen's Mother, 1897. © Akseli Gallen-Kallela
(1865/1931). Ateneum/The Antell Collection, Helsinki.
Photograph: The Central Art Archives.

Inkeri and Kylliki dressed in old style Finnish clothes.

Sibelius Park sculpture to the left of the head of Sibelius.

Helsinki street scene.

Parliament House in Helsinki with statue of Czar Alexander II.

World's largest wooden church at Kerimaki.

One of the farmhouses spared from the Nazi retreat in Rovaniemi, Lapland.

Windmill and riihi at a farm near Teuva.

Family items in attic.

Loom.

Old farm tools.

Carving of a peikko or troll. They are human-like beings that live in families or clans in woods, mountains, and hillocks.

Teuva symbol at entrance to folk festival.

Part IV

References, Bibliography, and Index

References

General

Chadwick, Owen. *A History of Christianity.* New York: St. Martin's Press, 1995.

Christiansen, Eric H., W. Kenneth Hamblin. *Exploring the Planets.* 2nd ed. Englewood Cliffs, NJ: Prentice-Hall, 1995.

Davies, Norman. *A History of Europe.* New York: Oxford University Press, 1996.

Dott, Robert H., Jr., Roger L. Batten. *Evolution of the Earth.* 3rd ed. New York: McGraw-Hill, 1981.

Doyle, Hugh. *Seismology.* New York: John Wiley and Sons, 1995.

Earth—The Science of Our Planet: Origins 7 no. 1 (February 1998). Waupesha, WI: Kambach Publishing.

Filkin, David. Foreword by Stephen Hawking. *Stephen Hawking's Universes: The Cosmos Explained.* New York: Basic Books, 1997.

Gallant, Roy A. *National Geographic Picture Atlas of Our Universe.* Washington, DC: National Geographic Society, 1994. pp. 284, 343.

Gonick, Larry. *The Cartoon History of the Universe: From the Big Bang to Alexander the Great.* 7 volumes. New York: Doubleday, 1990.

Jägerskiöld, Stig. *Mannerheim: Marshal of Finland.* Minneapolis: University of Minnesota Press, C. Hurst and Company Publishers, 1986.

Johnson, Jimmy, gen. ed. *What Makes the World Go Around?* New York: Henry Holt, 1997.

Jones, Gwyn. *A History of the Vikings.* 2nd ed. Oxford, England: Oxford University Press, 1984.

Newman, William L. *Geologic Time.* Washington, DC: U.S. Department of Interior/U.S. Geological Survey, 1996.

Sternglase, Ernest J. *Before the Big Bang: The Origins of the Universe.* New York: Four Walls Eight Windows, 1997.

Taylor, Barbara. *Earth Explained: A Beginner's Guide to Our Planet.* 1st ed. New York: Henry Holt, 1997.

Windley, Brian F. *The Evolving Continents.* 3rd ed. New York: John Wiley and Sons, 1995.

Finnish Geology

Taipale, Kalle, Jauko T. Parvianen. *Jokamiehen Geologia.* (Everyman's Geology). Helsinki, Finland: Kirjayhtymä OY, 1995.

Virkkunen, Marjatta, Seppo J. Partanen. *Suomen Kivet.* (The Rocks of Finland).

Selected Bibliography

Barraclough, Geoffrey, and Norman Stone, eds. *The Times Atlas of World History*, 3rd ed. Maplewood, NJ: Hammond, 1989.

Booss, Claire, ed. *Scandinavian Folk and Fairy Tales.* Avenel, NJ: Gramercy Books, 1984.

Bowman, James Cloyd, Margery Bianco, and Aili Kolehmainen. *Tales from a Finnish Tupa.* Chicago, IL: Albert Whitman, 1970.

Caraker, Mary. *Women of the Kalevala.* St. Cloud, MN: North Star Press, 1996.

Carlson, Bernice Wells, and Ristiina Wigg. *We Want Sunshine in Our House.* Nashville, TN: Abingdon Press, 1973.

Comrie, Bernard, Stephen Matthews, and Maria Polinsky, consulting eds. *The Atlas of Languages: The Origin and Development of Languages Throughout the World.* New York: Quarto, 1997.

Davies, Norman. *Europe: A History.* New York: Oxford University Press, 1996.

de Gerez, Toni. *Louhi, Witch of the North Farm.* Illustrated by Barbara Cooney. New York: Viking, 1986.

de Gerez, Tree. *When Bear Came Down from the Sky.* New York: Viking, 1994.

Deutsch, Babette. *Heroes of the Kalevala.* New York: Julian Messner, 1966.

Engle, Eloise, and Lauri Paananen. *The Winter War: The Russo-Finnish Conflict, 1939-1940.* New York: Scribner's, 1973.

Fillmore, Parker. *The Shepherd's Nosegay.* New York: Harcourt Brace Jovanovich, 1958.

Finland Handbook. Helsinki, Finland: Government Printing Centre and Finnish Tourist Board, 1992.

Friberg, Eino, trans. *The Kalevala, Epic of the Finnish People.* Keuruu, Finland: Otava Press, 1988.

Hoglund, A. William. *Finnish Immigrants in America, 1880-1920.* Madison, WI: University of Wisconsin Press, 1960.

Jutikkala, Eino, and Kauko Pirinen. *A History of Finland.* New York: Dorset Press, 1988.

Kirby, W. F., trans. *Kalevala, the Land of Heroes.* Volume I. New York: E. P. Dutton, 1961.

————, trans. *Kalevala, the Land of Heroes.* Volume II. London, England: J. M. Dent, 1962.

Kirkinen, Heikki, and Hannes Sihvo. *The Kalevala: An Epic of Finland and All Mankind.* Helsinki, Finland: Finnish-American Cultural Institute, 1985.

Kivikoski, E. *Finland: Ancient People and Places.* New York: Praeger, 1967.

Klinge, Matti. *A Brief History of Finland.* 10th ed. Helsinki, Finland: Otava Press, 1994.

————. *The Baltic World.* 2nd ed. Helsinki, Finland: Otava Press, 1994.

Kvideland, Reimund, and Henning K. Sehmsdorf, eds. *Scandinavian Folk Belief and Legend.* Minneapolis: University of Minnesota Press, 1988.

Lander, Patricia, and Claudette Charbonneau. *The Land and People of Finland.* New York: HarperCollins, 1990.

Layton, Robert. *Sibelius and His World.* New York: Viking Press, 1970.

Lewin, Ted. *The Reindeer People.* New York: Macmillan, 1994.

Lönnrot, Elias, comp., and Francis Peabody Magoun, Jr., trans. *The Kalevala.* Cambridge, MA: Harvard University Press, 1963.

Lönnrot, Elias, comp., and Keith Bosley, trans. *The Kalevala.* New York: Oxford University Press, 1989.

————. *The Kanteletar.* New York: Oxford University Press, 1992.

McNeil, M. E. A. *The Magic Storysinger.* Owings Mills, MD: Stemmer House, 1993.

Nickels, Sylvie, ed. *Finland: An Introduction.* New York: Praeger, 1968.

Pentikainen, Juha Y., and Ritva Poom, trans. *Kalevala Mythology.* Bloomington, IN: Indiana University Press, 1989.

Shepard, Aaron. *The Maiden of Northland.* New York: Atheneum, 1996.

Synge, Ursula. *Land of Heroes.* New York: Atheneum, 1978.

The Times Atlas of the World, 7th ed. New York: Times Books, 1988.

Troughton, Joanna. *The Magic Mill.* New York: Bedrick and Blackie, 1981.

Vuorela, Toivo. *The Finno-Ugric Peoples.* Volume 39. Bloomington, IN: Indiana University Press, 1964.

Index

Lore. *See* Folklore
Louhi, 82-89
Lures, 45
Lutefisk, 176
Lutheran Cathedral, 41
Lutheranism, 19

Maahinen, 63
Magic, 66, 67, 70
    drums, 16, 17, 65
Magic Fish of Gold, The, 96-100
Magic Mill, The, 82-89
Magic Millstone, The, 90-95
Magic Wish, The, 78-81
Main dishes, 173-77
Manala, 64
Mannerheim, Carl Gustaf, 27-28, 30
Marttinen, Martti, 31, 48
Marxists, 26
Master of the Gold, The, 163-68
May Day. *See* Vappu
Meatballs, 174
Medical lore, 67
Merimekko, 44
Metsanhaltija, 64
Mice, 161-62
Michigan, 32
Middle Ages, 15, 59
Midsummer Festival, 37
Mielikki, 63
Mills, 66
Millstones, 90-95
Mining, 32, 64
Minnesota, 32
Miss Finland, 30
Monsters. *See* Creatures
Montana, 32
Moral sayings, 55-58
Morton, John, 31

Mortonson, Morton, 31, 48
Museums, 42
Music, 39-40
Musical instruments, 36(fig.), 87-89
Musicians, 101-9
Myths. *See also* Folklore; Folktales
    creation, 6-7, 34
    sea, 59, 110-15

Nakki, 63, 127
Name Day, 37
Napoleonic Wars, 21
National epics, 69. *See also*
    Folktales
Natural resources, 14
Neptune, 62
Neva River, 14, 19
Nevanlinna, 19
New Year, 34, 46, 62
Nicholas II, 23-24, 26
Niebelungenlied, 69
Niilonpoika, Antti, 48
Noaide. *See* Shamanism
Nonalcoholic drinks, 181
North Sea, 9
Northern Lights. *See* Aurora
    Borealis
Norway, 9, 11
Novgorod, 14, 18. *See also* Russia
Nuutajarvi, 43

Oak trees, 7, 16, 44(fig.), 65
Olavinlinna Castle, 39, 42
Old Pagan, 141-43
Omenasilli, 176
Operas, 39
Ostrobothnia, 14, 27
Oven rice pudding, 180

About the Authors

Norma J. Livo is a retired professor of education at the University of Colorado, Denver. She is the author of many award-winning books on storytelling and folklore, a former National Storytelling Association board member, and past president of the Colorado Council of the International Reading Association. She is the recipient of the 1996 National Storytelling Association's Leadership Award and the 1995 Colorado Governor's Award for Excellence in the Arts.

George O. I. Livo is a retired geologist and geophysicist who had a successful career in worldwide oil and mineral exploration. He was born in Finland, but his formal education was in Canada and the United States. Outside activities include an extensive interest in archaeology, prehistory, and anthropology. He is presently involved in raising money for archaeological excavations at Amarna in Egypt.

Norma and George Livo. (Photograph courtesy Emmerich Photographers.)